THE WORKS 4

Pie Corbett and Gaby Morgan

Pie Corbett was a primary teacher and headteacher. He worked in teacher training and was English Inspector in Gloucestershire. He advised the National Literacy Strategy, especially on teaching poetry, writing and grammar. He writes training materials and runs in-service across the country. Author of over a hundred books, a poet and story-teller, he spends much of his time irritating editors by not answering the phone because he is making poems up or dreaming.

Gaby Morgan is the Editorial Director of the Macmillan Children's Books poetry list. She has edited a number of best-selling anthologies, including *Read Me: A Poem for Every Day of the Year* and *Christmas Poems*. She lives in Hampshire with Grant, Jude, Evie and Angel the cat.

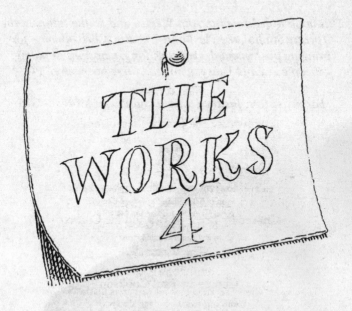

Every kind of poem on every
topic that you will ever need
for the literacy hour

Chosen by Pie Corbett
and Gaby Morgan

MACMILLAN CHILDREN'S BOOKS

This book is dedicated to Ann Wessen and all the tutors at the
'Theatre Studio', the Playhouse Theatre, Cheltenham – for
bringing poetry and drama alive for generations of young
people . ... and Daisy, who read these poems too. PC

For my sisters: Justine Dornan and Penny Morgan. GM

First published 2005 by Macmillan Children's Books
a division of Macmillan Publishers Limited
20 New Wharf Road, London N1 9RR
Basingstoke and Oxford
www.panmacmillan.com

Associated companies throughout the world

ISBN 0 330 43644 9

1 3 5 7 9 8 6 4 2

A CIP catalogue record for this book is available from the British Library.

Typeset by SX Composing DTP, Rayleigh, Essex
Printed and bound in Great Britain by Mackays of Chatham plc, Kent

Contents

A – The Ark and Other Creatures

B – Boys' Stuff

Contents

C – Celebrations and Festivals

Contents

D – Dinosaurs, Dragons and Dodos

E – Elements, Seasons and the Natural World

Contents

F – Friends and Families

Contents

G – Girls' Stuff

H – Home Life

Contents

I – Impossible and Incredible

J – Journeys

Contents

K – Kissing and Other Things Best Avoided

L – Love, Death, War and Peace

Contents

M – Monsters, Ghosts and Ghouls

Contents

N – Nonsense

O – Ourselves and Others

Contents

P – People and Places

Contents

Q – Queens, Kings and Historical Stuff

R – Rescuing the World

Contents

S – Senses and Feelings

Contents

T – Teachers

U – Unpleasant Things

Contents

V – Viewpoints

W – Wonder

Contents

X – X-words and Wordplay

Y – Young and Old

Contents

Z – Zapping Aliens

Contents

The Works 4 – Introduction

This alphabetical anthology collects together poems about a broad range of topics that interest young readers but do not fall under the National Curriculum. From 'dodos' to 'dragons' and 'disasters' to 'dreams', you will find poems about subjects that matter.

Many of the poems first appeared in the annual Macmillan World Book Day poetry anthologies and are now collected together for the first time. There are very few anthologies which give poets the chance to write about whatever matters to them – the sort of poems that had to be written. (Most anthologies are written by request – poems on typical subjects such as schools, animals or aliens.) But in this collection, we looked for poems on all sorts of topics, with no restrictions.

However, each poem had to earn its place – not just the glib grin or simplistic smirk, but poems that jolt the senses and make us feel alive. Kafka said that, 'one should only read books which bite and sting . . . If the book we are reading does not wake us up with a blow to the head, what's the point in reading? A book must be the axe which smashes the frozen sea within us.'

So, each poem here had to have that extra bite – to surprise, to challenge, to delight, to create wonder as well as the inexplicable charm of rhythmic and memorable language.

Pie Corbett and Gaby Morgan

At the back you will find indexes showing:

- different types of poem, so you can easily locate what you need – from 'haiku' to 'narrative poems';
- an alphabet for young poets about writing poetry;
- an alphabet of reading ideas;
- a glossary of poetic terms;
- teaching ideas for each section.

A

The Ark and Other Creatures

All Creatures

I just can't seem to help it,
I love creatures – great and small,
But it's ones that others do not like
I love the best of all.
I like creepy crawly beetles
And shiny black-backed bugs,
Gnats and bats and spiders,
And slimy fat black slugs.
I like chirpy little crickets
And buzzing bumblebees,
Lice and mice and ladybirds,
And tiny jumping fleas.
I like wasps and ants and locusts,
Centipedes and snails,
Moles and voles and earwigs
And rats with long pink tails,
I like giant moths with dusty wings
And maggots fat and white,
Worms and germs and weevils,
And fireflies in the night.
No, I just can't seem to help it,
To me not one's a pest,
It's ones that others do not like,
I seem to love the best.

So it makes it rather difficult,
It's enough to make me cry,
Because my job's in pest control,
And I just couldn't hurt a fly.

Gervase Phinn

Before the Days of Noah

Before the days of Noah
before he built his ark
seagulls sang like nightingales
and lions sang like larks.
The tortoise had a mighty roar
the cockerel had a moo
kitten always eeyored
and elephants just mewed.
It was the way the world was
. . . when owls had a bark
and dogs did awful crowings
whilst running round the park.

Horses baaaed like baa lambs
ducks could all miaow
and animals had voices
quite different from now!
But, came the day of flooding
and all the world was dark
the animals got weary
of living in the ark –
So they swapped around their voices
a trumpet for a mew
– a silly sort of pastime
when nothing much to do.
But when the flood had ended
and the world was nice and dry
the creatures had forgotten
how once they hissed or cried.

So they kept their brand-new voices
– forgot the days before
– when lions use to giggle
and gerbils used to roar.

Peter Dixon

Mary Had a Crocodile

Mary had a crocodile
That ate a child each day;
But interfering people came
And took her pet away.

Anon.

Cows on the Beach

Two cows,
fed-up with grass, field, farmer,
barged through barbed wire
and found the beach.
Each mooed to each:
This is a better place to be,
a stretch of sand next to the sea,
this is the place for me.
And they stayed there all day,
strayed this way, that way,
over to rocks,
past discarded socks,
ignoring the few people they met
(it wasn't high season yet).
They dipped hooves in the sea,
got wet up to the knee,
they swallowed pebbles and sand,

found them a bit bland,
washed them down the sea-water,
decided they really ought to
rest for an hour.
Both where sure
they'd never leave here.
Imagine, they'd lived so near
and never knew!
With a swapped moo
they sank into sleep,
woke to the yellow jeep
of the farmer
revving there
feet from the incoming sea.
This is no place for cows to be,
he shouted, and slapped them
with seaweed, all the way home.

Matthew Sweeney

The Cow

The friendly cow, all red and white,
I love with all my heart:
She gives me cream with all her might,
To eat with apple-tart.

She wanders lowing here and there,
And yet she cannot stray,
All in the pleasant open air,
The pleasant light of day;

And blown by all the winds that pass
And wet with all the showers,
She walks among the meadow grass
And eats the meadow flowers.

Robert Louis Stevenson

Water trough

Water trough
a horse
drinking sky

ai li

Claws

If my cat
were a fish, he'd be a shark.
A big shark.
A big, mean shark.
A Great White Shark.

But he's not a fish.
He's a cat.
A big cat.
A big, mean cat.
A Great White Cat

who cruises the neighbourhood
terrorizing any creature
he happens to meet.

Birds wing away
when he prowls the gardens.
Other cats scat
when he struts his stuff
and even dogs make sure
they're somewhere else
when he's around.

He's rough. He's tough.
He's terrible to behold.
More terrible
than any tiger.

Sometimes he disappears
for days and days
and days

but just when
I start to think
I'll never see him again

in he strolls
pushing through the cat-flap
as if he's never been away

and he jumps up
into my lap
and curls himself
around himself

and falls asleep
purring like a Porsche
while I stroke him
and stroke him

and tell him
over and over again
that he's

the Best Cat
in the Whole Universe.

Tony Langham

Barry's Budgie . . . Beware!

Dave's got a dog the size of a lion
Half-wolf, half-mad, frothing with venom
It chews up policemen and then spits them out
But it's nothing to the bird I'm talking about.

Claire's got a cat as wild as a cheetah
Scratching and hissing, draws blood by the litre
Jumps high walls and hedges, fights wolves on its own
But there's one tough budgie it leaves well alone.

Murray my eel has teeth like a shark
Don't mess with Murray, he'll zap out a spark
But when Barry's budgie flies over the houses
Murray dims down his lights, blows his own fuses.

This budgie's fierce, a scar down its cheek
Tattoos on its wings, a knife in its beak
Squawks wicked words, does things scarcely legal
Someone should tell Barry it's really an eagle.

David Harmer

Old Man Platypus

Far from the trouble and toil of town,
Where the reed-beds sweep and shiver,
Look at a fragment of velvet brown –
Old Man Platypus drifting down,
Drifting along the river.

And he plays and dives in the river bends
In a style that is most elusive;
With few relations and fewer friends,
For Old Man Platypus descends
From a family most exclusive.

He shares his burrow beneath the bank
With his wife and his son and daughter
At the roots of the reeds and the grasses rank;
And the bubbles show where our hero sank
To its entrance under water.

Safe in their burrow below the falls
They live in a world of wonder,
Where no one visits and no one calls,
They sleep like little brown billiard balls
With their beaks tucked neatly under.

And he talks in a deep unfriendly growl
As he goes on his journey lonely;
For he's no relation to fish nor fowl,
Nor to bird nor beast, nor to horned owl;
In fact, he's the one and only!

A. B. Paterson

Weary Will the Wombat

The strongest creature for his size
But least equipped for combat
That dwells beneath Australian skies
Is Weary Will the Wombat.

He digs his homestead underground,
He's neither shrewd nor clever;
For kangaroos can leap and bound
But wombats dig for ever.

The boundary-rider's netting fence
Excites his irritation;
It is to his untutored sense
His pet abomination.

And when to pass it he desires,
Upon his task he'll centre
And dig a hole beneath the wires
Through which the dingoes enter.

And when to block the hole they strain
With logs and stones and rubble,
Bill Wombat digs it out again
Without the slightest trouble.

The boundary-rider bows to fate,
Admits he's made a blunder,
And rigs a little swinging gate
To let Bill Wombat under.

So most contentedly he goes
Between his haunt and burrow:
He does the only thing he knows,
And does it very thorough.

A. B. Paterson

Larks with Sharks

I love to go swimming when a great shark's about,
I tease him by tickling his tail and his snout
With the ostrich's feather I'm never without
And when I start feeling those glinty teeth so close
With a scrunchy snap snap on my ankles or toes
I swim off with a laugh (for everyone knows
An affectionate nip from young sharky just shows
How dearly he loves every bit of his friend),
And when I've no leg just a stumpy chewed end
I forgive him for he doesn't mean to offend;
When he nuzzles my head, he never intends
With his teeth so delightfully set out in rows
To go further than rip off an ear or a nose,
But when a shark's feeling playful, why, anything goes!
With tears in his eyes he'll take hold of my arm
Then twist himself round with such grace and such charm
The bits slip down his throat – no need for alarm!
I've another arm left! He means me no harm!

He'll play stretch and snap with six yards of insides
The rest will wash up on the beach with the tides
What fun we've all had, what a day to remember –
Yes, a shark loves a pal he can slowly dismember.

David Orme

Rhinos and Roses

When more than one rhinoceros
Becomes rhinoceroses, and each of these
has horns of hair that stick up from their
noses, and armoured skin that wallows in
the mud when they reposes, and on each
foot each rhino has three hoofs
instead of toeses – the features
of these creatures show becomes
the problem
language poses
when more rhinoc-
than one
rhinoceros er oses.

Gina Douthwaite

Tiger

A colour splasher
A stripe flasher
An eye gleamer
A wide beamer
A sleek sprinter
A smart hunter
A lone prowler
A loud growler
A night walker
A deer stalker
A soft sneaker
A strong striker
A swift pouncer
A quick bouncer
A fierce snarler
A cruel mauler
A great fighter
A bad biter
A meat eater
A man hater

Usha Kishore

The Royal Bengal Tiger is the national animal of Bangladesh and India.

children panicking

Children panicking
out of the tiger cage
a wasp

David Cobb

Rat It Up

C'mon everybody
Slap some grease on those paws
Get some yellow on your teeth
And, uh, sharpen up your claws

There's a whole lot of sausage
We're gonna swallow down
We're going to jump out the sewers
And rock this town

Cos we're ratting it up
Yes we're ratting it up
Well we're ratting it up
For a ratting good time tonight

Ain't got no compass
You don't need no map
Just follow your snout
Hey, watch out for that trap!

You can take out a poodle
You can beat up a cat
But if you can't lick a ferret
You ain't no kind of rat

Cos we're ratting it up
Yes we're ratting it up
Well we're ratting it up
For a ratting good time tonight

Now you can sneak in the henhouse
Roll out the eggs
But if the farmer comes running
Bite his hairy legs

Check that cheese for poison
Before you eat
Or you'll wind up being served up
As ratburger meat

Cos we're ratting it up
Yes we're ratting it up
Well we're ratting it up
For a ratting good time tonight

This rat was born to rock
This rat was born to roll
I don't give a monkey's
Bout your pest control

So push off pussy-cat
Push off pup
We're the Rockin' Rodents
And we're ratting it up

Yeah we're ratting it up
Yeah we're ratting it up
Well we're ratting it up
For a ratting good time tonight!

Adrian Mitchell

Lock the Dairy Door!

Old Fox comes trotting over the hill
　　Down from Caistor Tor,
On through the woods by the water-mill.
　　Lock the dairy door!

He's an orange flame in the early light
　　As he sneaks between the trees,
With his tail down low and his sharp eyes bright
　　He sniffs the morning breeze.

Near to the farm he drops his speed.
  Head to the ground he goes.
These are hungry cubs in the den to feed.
  He twitches his clever nose.

The proud cock struts by the chicken run,
  Raises his head to the sky,
And lifts his voice to the morning sun,
  With, 'Fly, sisters, fly!'

'Fly, sisters. Fly!
  To the perch in the old grain store.
A hungry fox is passing by.
  Lock the dairy door!'

Old Fox goes trotting past the farm
  Turns north, toward his lair.
Now no chicken will come to harm
  But rabbits – beware!

Gerard Benson

Midnight Meeting

On soft, silent, padded paws,
all cats are grey in the night;
this is their time.

A shadow walking in shadows,
Prometheus is on the prowl.
Other toms keep their distance,
and a fox crosses the road
to avoid him;
but the mouse saw nothing,
heard nothing,
knew nothing.

On wings without a whisper,
old Tawny perches
on the chimney pot,
in time to see the cat
snatch his prey.
Their eyes meet,
the owl and the pussycat,
the staring match of all time.

Prometheus looks away first.
After all,
he has the mouse.

Mike Jubb

Animal Riddle

Like a small Bear
                bundles over the dark road,
     brushes pAst the front gate,
          as if she owns the joint.
     rolls the Dustbin,
              like an expert barrel rider,
tucks into yesterday's Garbage,
          crunches worms for titbits.
   wakes us from dEep sleep,
          blinks back at torchlight.
  our midnight feasteR,
         ghost-friend,
         moon-lit,
         zebra bear.

Pie Corbett

Barn Owl

Captured, the barn owl will slump
in its cage, a corner of dead feathers
propped like a crumpled pillow.
It sags, almost heart-stopped, its fly-by-night
moth-flight a dream, hallucination
of moon's full breath falling on the flying fields,
and life as silent as surprise,
as easy as the focus of the eye and catch of ear.

And now the torn wing screeches
in the mop-and-bucket clatter of the feeding dish,
all stainless steel and sawdust reeking,
the dead chick offered limply at the beak in tweezers.
The night behind his eyes darkens,
he fights the squeeze of his resisting beak,
then gulps and swallows the only way back.

Judith Green

B

Boys' Stuff

What Are Little Boys Made of?

What are little boys made of, made of?
What are little boys made of?
  Frogs and snails
  And puppy-dogs' tails.
That's what little boys are made of.

Anon.

We Are the Year Six Boys

We're the boys in Year Six
And we are cool
The coolest class
In the school

We don't raise a smile
We don't make a fuss
There's no one as cool
As cool as us

We stand in the playground
We talk about stuff
We walk very slowly
Because we are tough

We saunter, we hang
We are nobody's fool
We're the boys in Year Six
And we are the cool

Roger Stevens

When Is a Boy Not a Boy?

For Oswald and Selhurst Boys

When is a boy not a boy?
When he's a plank of wood.

When is a boy a plank of wood?
When he goes rigid with fear.

When does a boy go rigid with fear?
When he's being carried across the river.

When is a boy carried across the river?
When he's the smallest in a party of boys being chased by
   bullocks.

*When is a boy part of a party of boys being chased by
   bullocks?*
When they're being taken for a walk to the nearest village
   by their history teacher.

27

*When is a boy taken for a walk to the nearest village by his
history teacher?*
When he's staying in a thatched farmhouse to do creative
writing in the middle of Devon.

*When does a boy stay in a thatched farmhouse to do
creative writing in the middle of Devon?*
When he's capable of becoming a plank of wood.

Chrissie Gittins

A Visit to Yalding

We went to Yalding to look at the locks
To watch the water going up and down.
My brother found a dead sparrow to take home,
My mum found a ten pence piece,
My dad picked up a tin can that an animal might hurt itself on
And I –
I fell in the river.

I dripped back to the car.
'You're not getting into the car like that,'
said Dad. 'You'll ruin the upholstery.'
'You're not getting into the car like that,'
said Mum. 'You'll catch your death of cold.
Get those wet things off.'
I took off my squelchy shoes.

I took off my soggy socks.
And stopped.
'And the rest,' said Mum.
'No, Mum, please.'
'No one will see.'
'I can see,' said my brother
'No looking.'
Off came the saturated shorts.
'I can see his pants.
I can see his pants.
And they're wet,' said my brother helpfully.

'They're not.'
'Get them off,' said Mum.
'No, Mum, please.'
'Don't be such a big drip.
Are you going to take them off
Or shall I?'
Down came the pants.
I sat on a towel in the car
next to my brother who was near wetting himself
    with laughter.
'What's it like to
What's it like to
What's it like to
have no pants?'

'Mum. Tell him.
Mum?
Dad?
Stop laughing.
It's not funny.'
'You're right,' said Dad.
There was a moment's silence
Then they all started laughing again.
Could my life ever reach a lower ebb?
It did at the end of our road.

'Oh. Isn't that Pamela Whitehorn?'
said my brother.
'Where?'
I looked.
It was.
'You love her.'
'I don't.'
'Do. Otherwise you wouldn't be blushing.'
'I'm not blushing.
People always go red when they've fallen in the river
Everybody knows that.'
'Shall I tell her you haven't got any pants on?'
'You dare.'
'That's enough,' said Mum.

The shame.
Pantless before Pamela.

Through the window, I peeped at Pamela.
She was looking right at me.
Pamela knew things.
She knew where babies came from.
I wondered whether boys sitting in cars with no
    pants on
Looked any different to boys sitting in cars with
    pants on.
I waved in a casual 'I've got my pants on' sort of way.
If there was a difference
Pamela would know.

John Coldwell

Monday Morning 10.00 a.m.

At times like these
he dreams of being
somewhere else
altogether

More often
than not
he's out
in space
freefloating
over the earth
watching the clouds
twist and twirl
over the great
blue oceans

Anything
to get out
of double maths

James Carter

Our Ditch

I sat and thought one day
of all the things we'd done
with our ditch; how we'd jumped across
at its tightest point, till I slipped
and fell, came out smelling,
then laid a pole from side to side,
dared each other to slide along it.
We fetched out things that others threw in,
lobbed bricks at tins, played Pooh-sticks.
We buried stuff in the mud and the gunge
then threatened two girls with a ducking.
We floated boats and bombed them,
tiptoed along when the water was ice
till something began to crack, and we scuttled back.
We borrowed Mum's sieve from the baking drawer,
scooped out tadpoles into a jar
then simply forgot to put them back.
(We buried them next to the cat.)
Then one slow day in summer heat
we followed our ditch to where it began,
till ditch became stream, and stream
fed river, and river slopped off to the sea.
Strange, we thought, our scrap of water
growing up and leaving home,
roaming the world and lapping
at distant lands.

Brian Moses

Den to Let

To let
One self-contained
Detached den.
Accommodation is compact
Measuring one yard square.
Ideal for two eight-years-olds
Plus one small dog
Or two cats
Or six gerbils.
Accommodation consists of:
One living-room
Which doubles as kitchen
Bedroom
Entrance-hall
Dining-room
Dungeon
Space capsule
Pirate boat
Covered wagon
Racing car
Palace
Aeroplane
Junk-room
And lookout post.

Property is southward facing
And can be found
Within a short walking distance

Of the back door
At bottom of garden.
Easily found in the dark
By following the smell
Of old cabbages and tea-bags.
Convenient escape routes
Past rubbish dump
To Seager's Lane
Through hole in hedge,
Or into next door's garden;
But beware of next door's rhinoceros
Who sometimes thinks he's a poodle.

Construction is of
Sound corrugated iron
And roof doubles as shower
During rainy weather.
Being partially underground,
Den makes
A particularly effective hiding place
When in a state of war
With older sisters
Brothers
Angry neighbours
Or when you simply want to be alone.
Some repair work needed
To north wall
Where Mr Spence's foot came through
When planting turnips last Thursday.

With den go all contents
Including:
One carpet – very smelly
One teapot – cracked
One woolly penguin –
No beak and only one wing
One unopened tin
Of sultana pud
One hundred and three Beanos
Dated 1983–1985
And four Rupert annuals.
Rent is free
The only payment being
That the new occupant
Should care for the den
In the manner to which it has been accustomed
And on long Summer evenings
Heroic songs of days gone by
Should be loudly sung
So that old and glorious days
Will never be forgotten.

Gareth Owen

I Would Win the Gold if These Were Olympic Sports . . .

Bubble gum blowing
Goggle box watching
Late morning snoring
Homework botching

Quilt ruffling
Little brother teasing
Pizza demolishing
Big toe cheesing

Insult hurling, wobbly throwing
Infinite blue belly button fluff growing

Late night endurance computer screen gazing
Non-attentive open-jawed eyeball glazing

Ultimate volume decibel blaring
Long-distance marathon same sock wearing

Recognise all these as sports then meet . . .
Me! The Champ Apathetic Athlete!

Paul Cookson

He Just Can't Kick It with His Foot

John Luke from our team
Is a goal-scoring machine
Phenomenally mesmerizing but . . .
The sport is called football
But his boots don't play at all
Cos he just can't kick it with his foot.

He can skim it from his shin
He can spin it on his chin
He can nod it in the net with his nut
He can blow it with his lips
Or skip it off his hips
But he just can't kick it with his foot

With simplicity and ease
He can use his knobbly knees
To blast it past the keeper, both eyes shut
He can whip and flick it
Up with his tongue and lick it
But he still can't kick it with his foot

Overshadowing the best
With the power from his chest
Like a rocket from a socket he can put
The ball into the sack
With a scorcher from his back
But he just can't kick it with his foot

Baffling belief
With the ball between his teeth
He can dribble his way out of any rut
Hypnotize it with his eyes
Keep it up on both his thighs
But he just can't kick it with his foot

From his shoulder to his nose
He can juggle it and pose
With precision and incision he can cut
Defences straight in half
With a volley from his calf
But he just can't kick it with his foot

He can keep it off the deck
Bounce the ball upon his neck
With his ball control you should see him strut
He can flap it with both ears
To loud applause and cheers
But he just can't kick it with his foot

He can trap it with his tum
Direct it with his bum
Deflect it just by wobbling his gut
When he's feeling silly
He can even use his . . . ankle
But he just can't kick it with his foot.

Paul Cookson

Match of the Year

I am delivered to the stadium by chauffeur-driven
  limousine.
Gran and Grandpa give me a lift in their Mini.

I change into my sparkling clean world-famous designer
  strip.
*I put on my brother's shorts and the T-shirt with tomato
  ketchup stains.*

I give my lightweight professional boots a final shine.
I rub the mud off my trainers.

The coach gives me a final word of encouragement.
Dave, the sports master, tells me to get a move on.

I jog calmly through the tunnel out into the stadium.
I walk nervously onto the windy sports field.

The crowd roars.
Gran and Grandpa shout, 'There's our Jimmy!'

The captain talks last-minute tactics.
'Pass to me or I'll belt you.'

The whistle goes. The well-oiled machine goes into action.
Where did the ball go?

I pass it skilfully to our international star, Bernicci.
I kick it away. Luckily, Big Bernard stops it before it goes over the line.

A free kick is awarded to the visiting Premier team. I'm part of the impregnable defence.
The bloke taking the kick looks six feet tall – and just as wide . . .

I stop the ball with a well-timed leap and head it expertly up the field.
The ball thwacks me on the head.

The crowd shouts my name! 'Jim-meee! Jim-meee! Jim-meee!'
Gran says, 'Eee, our Jim's fallen over.'

I don't remember any more.

Trevor Millum

who knows about UFOs?

If **UFOs** are Unidentified Flying Objects –
whose job is it to identify them?

And, once identified, does a **UFO** become an **IFO**?

And, if a **UFO** can no longer fly –
perhaps due to a technical problem –
does it become a **UO**?

And, if I threw my slipper in the air –
and nobody knew what it was –
would it too be a **UFO**?

I think I'll file these questions under
Utterly Fantastic ObservationS

James Carter

Night Train

The train
is a shiny caterpillar
in clackety boots
nosing through the blind night,
munching mile after mile
of darkness

Irene Rawnsley

Shaking the Branches

(A Boy's War Poem)

I'm shaking our walnut tree,
standing in its fork,
and I can see for miles.

A farmer is ploughing
with one piebald horse.
And the crows are flying.

It's not a school day.
The sun, low on the horizon
is bright in my eyes.

My fingers are stained
with walnut juice;
my bare knees are cold.

There are apples in the barrel
and tomatoes on the sill;
and on the range, a juicy stew.

The swallows have gone
and smoke is curling
from the barley-sugar chimneys.

My parents are a hundred
miles away in a bombed city.
Churchill is on the news,

and I am standing in the fork
of a walnut tree
shaking the branches.

Gerard Benson

C

Celebrations and Festivals

A Birthday Poem For Rachel

For every year of life we light
a candle on your cake
to mark the simple sort of progress
anyone can make,
and then, to test your nerve or give
a proper view of death,
you're asked to blow each light, each year,
out with your own breath.

James Simmons

The Moon at Knowle Hill

The Moon was married last night
and nobody saw
dressed up in her ghostly dress
for the summer ball.

The stars shimmied in the sky
and danced a whirligig;
the moon vowed to be true
and lit up the corn-rigs.

She kissed the dark lips of the sky
above the summer house,
she in her pale white dress
swooned across the vast sky.

The moon was married last night,
the beautiful belle of the ball,
and nobody saw her at all
except a small girl in a navy dress

who witnessed it all.

Jackie Kay

Mehndi *Time*

(To welcome Tulika to our family)

The love of family and friends –
at *mehndi* time, at *mehndi* time –
the joy of stories and laughter –
at *mehndi* time, at *mehndi* time,
embrace me like a magic ring
as they clap their hands and sing:

May the new bride bring a blessing,
mehndi magic mark her wedding.
With designs – intricate and neat –
we'll decorate her hands and feet.

With bright lines of ochre colour –
at *mehndi* time, at *mehndi* time –
my sisters pattern loving warmth –
at *mehndi* time, at *mehndi* time.
In life my journey may be far
as I pursue my *mehndi* star.

Painted shells and lotus flowers
decorate these happy hours.
Rich mango leaves and tree of life –
love's anchors grace our new-wed wife.

I will nourish tradition's fruit
at *mehndi* time, at *mehndi* time.
What memories I will cherish –
at *mehndi* time, at *mehndi* time!
Like *mehndi* bushes, cool and green,
may *mehndi* make my life serene.

Her feet are tinted coral-rose,
her hands are jewels in repose.
May her new life flow with blessing,
mehndi magic mark her wedding.

It's *mehndi* time, it's *mehndi* time . . .

Debjani Chatterjee

mehndi: henna.

Christening Gift

The gift I bestow is last but not least –
A permanent magical feast,
A path to knowledge, a key to learning
That grows with you at each year's turning,
A thousand stories for your pleasure,
Jokes and prayers in equal measure,
Conversation and songs for singing,
Poems for the joy of wild words ringing.
I grant you a life spent under its spell.
Words are my gift – use them well.

Sue Cowling

Come Play with Me – it's Holi!

Come play with me
it's Holi!

Tell me you won't play
and I'll pelt you anyway
with colours that will stay
with you all day – for today
is Holi!

You are the girl that didn't care
to throw a glance at me.
I am the boy that didn't dare
to ask you to dance with me.

Today I'm out with my gang
drenched with colour, drunk with *bhang*
I am your Krishna come to play
your friends – my *Gopis* who will spray
me with *abir*, for today
is Holi!

And you my Radha cannot stay inside.
The spring sky calls, come play outside
with coloured water – do not hide –
for today is Holi!

Upset the coloured powder mounds
in clouds of purple, pink and green,
let your *chunni* swirl around,
join your bangled hands with hand.

It's true I do not have a flute
or peacock feathers on my head;
I only know the Bombay hits
and have a cricket cap instead,
which I will throw at your feet
and dance the *bhangra* to the beat
as we sway our hips today
to the *dholki*'s frenzied beat . . .

Rhythmic shoulders, clapping hands,
faces streaked, coloured strands,
saris sprayed, *kurtas* stained
friends doused, strangers drained
from pistons, buckets, balconies,
street corners, terraces and trees –
till the wall you try to build
crumbles down against my will

I'll touch your cheeks and arms
with colour which disarms
you for one day
of abandon –
so let us play
as Radha-Krishna – for today
is Holi!

Bashabi Fraser

Holi: Hindu spring festival of colours.

Bhang: an alcoholic drink that is drunk at Holi. It is made with milk, nuts and herbs.

Krishna: a popular god who has a peacock feather in his hair and plays the flute enchantingly. He loved to dance with the Gopis or milkmaids, chief among whom was his sweetheart Radha.

Abir: the coloured powder with which Holi is played.

Chunni: a scarf worn over a blouse and hair.

Bhangra: a Punjabi folk dance.

Dholki: a kind of drum.

Kurtas: long tunics worn in India and Pakistan.

A Card for Me Mom

It is Mother's Day tomorrow
and the shops are full of wonderful things –
candles, picture-frames, potpourri in glass dishes,
but I only have money for a card, and there are dozens –
cards with teddies and roses, cards with moms
in dresses, with gold and red hair and blue eyes.
None of them look like me Mom.
If there was just one card to show
Mom with her gold necklace, bangles and earrings,
reminding me of her soft jingle-jangle as she washes
the curry pots or mixes the dough for *rotis* and *naans*,
in her silk *kameezes* and chiffon *chunnies* – one mom
with long black hair and flashing dark eyes
who looks more like me Mom!

Bashabi Fraser

Kameez: a long tunic dress worn by South Asian women over a *salwar* (trousers).
Roti: a flat round bread cooked on a griddle.
Naan: baked bread for Pakistan and North India.
Chunni: a long scarf worn over a *kameez*.

Mother's Day

Dear God,
Today is Mother's Day.
Please may her backache go away.

May her pot plants all grow healthy
and a win on the lottery make her wealthy.

May our dad buy her some flowers
and take us all to Alton Towers.

May her fruitcake always rise
and the sun shine bright
in her blue skies.

Protect her, God, she's growing old
And keep her warm.
(She feels the cold)

Roger Stevens

Easter Monday

We tied the white eggs in onion skin,
Wrapped them round with string.
We boiled them for so long
The water looked like strong tea.
Lifted out, the string was a dirty khaki,
But the eggs – the eggs were glorious
Marbled brown, amber and yellow.

When we were at the top of the hill,
When the others rolled theirs down to crack,
I held mine back –
It was too beautiful.

Catherine Benson

Ramadan

The moon that once was full, ripe and golden,
Wasted away, thin as the rind of a melon,
Like those poor whom sudden ill fortune
Has wasted away like a waning moon.

Like the generous who leave behind
All that was selfish and unkind,
The moon comes out of the tent of the night
And finds its way with a lamp of light.

The lamp of the moon is relit
And the hungry and thirsty
In the desert or the city
Make a feast to welcome it.

Stanley Cook

The Pumpkin Head

After the trickntreating children,
half-scared and full of sweets,
have hopped on doorsteps for another year,
the pumpkin head grins sharply
from its carved lopsided mouth
wry in the kitchen, drying out:
soup ebbing from the bowl an ochre tide
and pumpkin pie decreasing as the wedge-shaped days go by
to Bonfire Night.

Then finally, spent rockets rotting on the sodden ground,
you spear the pumpkin head
on tee-peed sweet-pea sticks.
And in November afternoons it floats,
a ghoulish apparition in the gathering dark
for passing cats to glance at, then hurry on
as if they recognise some primitive art
or warning.

Judith Green

Divali

Winter stalks us
like a leopard in the mountains
scenting prey.

It grows dark,
bare trees stick black bars
across the moon's silver eye.

I will light my lamp for you
Lakshmi,
drive away the darkness.

Welcome you into my home
Lakshmi,
beckon you from every window

With light that blazes
out like flames
across the sombre sky.

Certain houses
crouch in shadow, do not hear
your gentle voice.

Will not feel
your gentle heartbeat
bring prosperity and fortune.

Darkness hunts them
like a leopard in the mountains
stalking prey.

David Harmer

Fireworks

They rise like sudden fiery flowers
   That burst upon the night,
Then fall to earth in burning showers
   Of crimson, blue, and white.

Like buds too wonderful to name,
   Each miracle unfolds,
And catherine-wheels begin to flame
   Like whirling marigolds.

Rockets and Roman candles make
   An orchard of the sky.
Whence magic trees their petals shake
   Upon each gazing eye.

James Reeves

Fire at Night

It's ready steady sticks for fiery fun,
The strike of the match is the starter's gun.
Up go the flames, long-jumping sky,
The smoke catches up, hurdling high.
The crowd stamp their frozen feet
Clap their hands for the winning heat.
Guy Fawkes sits on top of the pyre,
Easily beaten, eaten by fire.
Who is the quickest in the scorching race?
Flames of gold grab first place.
Who beat the day? The crowd then roars
The moon made silver to the stars' applause.
Who has come third? No one remembers,
As they all sprint home, leaving only bronze embers.
As clouds shuffle by with a marathon creep,
Children in bed clutch the prize of sleep.

Andrew Fusek Peters

Thanksgiving

Thank You
for all my hands can hold –
apples red,
and melons gold,
yellow corn
both ripe and sweet,
peas and beans
so good to eat!

Thank You
for all my eyes can see –
lovely sunlight,
field and tree,
white cloud-boats
in sea-deep sky,
soaring bird
and butterfly.

Thank You
for all my ears can hear –
birds' song echoing
far and near,
songs of little
stream, big sea,
cricket, bullfrog,
duck and bee!

Ivy O. Eastwick

Light the Festive Candles

(For Hanukkah)

Light the first of eight tonight –
the farthest candle to the right.

Light the first and second, too,
when tomorrow's day is through.

Then light three, and then light four –
every dusk one candle more

Till at eight burn bright and high,
honouring a day gone by

When the Temple was restored,
rescued from the Syrian lord

And an eight-day feast proclaimed –
The Festival of Lights – well named

To celebrate the joyous day
when we regained the right to pray
to our one God in our own way.

Aileen Fisher

*The Jewish festival of Hanukkah lasts eight days, and on each day a
candle is lit in a special holder called a Menorah. The festival celebrates
the Syrians being driven out of Jerusalem and the Jews regaining their
freedom to worship in the Temple.*

Just Doing My Job

I'm one of Herod's Henchmen.
We don't have much to say,
We just charge through the audience
In a Henchman sort of way.

We all wear woolly helmets
To hide our hair and ears,
And wellingtons sprayed silver
To match our tinfoil spears.

Our swords are made of cardboard
So blood will not be spilled
If we trip and stab a parent
When the hall's completely filled.

We don't look VERY scary,
We're mostly small and shy,
And some of us wear glasses,
But we give the thing a try.

We whisper Henchman noises
While Herod hunts for strangers,
And then we all charge out again
Like nervous Power Rangers.

Yet when the play is over
And Miss is out of breath
We'll charge like Henchmen through the hall
And scare our Mums to death.

Clare Bevan

The First Christmas

It never snows at Christmas
in that dry and dusty land.
Instead of freezing blizzards,
there are palms and drifting sands
and years ago, a stable
and above, a glorious star
and three wise men who followed it
on camels, from afar,
while, sleepy on the quiet hills,
a shepherd gave a cry.
He'd seen a crowd of angels
in the silent, starlit sky.
In the stable, ox and ass stood
very still and calm,
gazing at the baby
safe and snug in Mary's arms.
But Joseph, lost in shadow,
face lit by an oil lamp's glow,
stood wondering, that first Christmas day,
two thousand years ago.

Marian Swinger

On the Thirteenth Day of Christmas My True Love Phoned Me Up . . .

Well, I suppose I should be grateful, you've
    obviously gone
to a lot of trouble and expense – or maybe off
    your head.
Yes, I did like the birds – the small ones anyway
    were fun
if rather messy, but now the hens have roosted on
    my bed
and the rest are nested on the wardrobe. It's hard
    to sleep
with all that cooing, let alone the cackling of the geese
whose eggs are everywhere, but mostly in a broken
    smelly heap
on the sofa. No, why should I mind? I can't get
    any peace
anywhere – the lounge is full of drummers
    thumping tom-toms
and sprawling lords crashed out from manic leaping.
    The kitchen
is crammed with cows and milkmaids and smells
    of a million stink-bombs
and enough sour milk to last a year. The pipers?
    I'd forgotten them –
they were no trouble, I paid them and they went.
    But I can't get rid

of these young ladies. They won't stop dancing or
　　turn the music down
and they're always in the bathroom, squealing as
　　they skid
across the flooded floor. No, I don't need a
　　plumber round,
it's just the swans – where else can they swim?
　　Poor things,
I think they're going mad, like me. When I went
　　to wash my
hands one ate the soap, another swallowed the
　　gold rings.
And the pear tree died. Too dry. So thanks for
　　nothing, love. Goodbye.

Dave Calder

One Christmas Wish?

For snow
to fall all Christmas Eve
in thick, slow flakes;
to fall all through
the hours I drift
in my warm bed
dreaming of Christmas Day.

For snow to lie
next morning
deep and soft;
for me to wake
and see the world
dressed as I've never
seen it dressed
in Christmas white.

For me to plant
my first time footprints
like a new astronaut
on a new moon;
to snowball slide,
shout loud 'hallo-oo-oo-s'
through the crisp air;
build snowmen
with red berry lips,
holly green hair.

Later, inside,
to curl up on the rug;
hear grown-ups talk
of snow adventures
Christmases ago.

One wish,
for one white Christmas
– one –
before *I'm* old.

Patricia Leighton

D

Dinosaurs, Dragons and Dodos

Some Other Ark

Two by two
the animals everybody knows
trotted, slithered,

hopped or were carried
up Noah's gangplank.
But there was some other ark

the unicorns chose:
an ill-pitched ark of bad gopher,
and ark that leaked,

The man who sailed it couldn't
smell or taste wind or rain
or see the Pole Star's crawl.

He missed all olive leaves.
Drowned dragons, griffins, phoenixes
and my precious unicorns.

Fred Sedgwick

To See a Unicorn

This is the way to see a Unicorn:

Close your eyes.

See a sandy path in front of you.
Follow that path over a hill of grass and daises.

Take a deep breath.
See a bumpy little stream in front of you.

Follow that stream into a forest.
Take a deep breath.

See a clearing in the forest
And a pool like a mirror for the trees.

Take a deep breath.
Be still.

Who walks so gracefully down to the pool
And bends to drink the cool dark water?

It is the Unicorn, the loveliest of animals.
He loves to wander in the forest of your dream

See his silver mane and his golden horn.
See his gentle eyes.
Hear the beating of his heart.

Be still.

Open your eyes
When you want to open your eyes.

Remember the Unicorn.

Adrian Mitchell

The Last Mountain

Once we mountains sported wings,
soared proud above the heavens,
frolicked among fleecy clouds
and slid up and down the rainbows
that groaned with our mighty weight.
Rushing wind was our element;
we played the music of the spheres.
The sky gifted us a giddy lightness
that stole the breath away.
But we took our freedom for granted
and jealous gods have clipped our wings.
Now distant thunder growls our grumbles
as my brothers and sisters tower in dreams
of how we once were monarchs of the air.
But I, the smallest of the mountains,
escaped the wrath of gods.
I hide in the frothing ocean and, sleepless,

I bide my time with folded wings.
The sea soil rumbles my secret songs
as I call to my family to take heart.
Their trust will strengthen me
and lift me up to strike a blow for our kind,
to fly up to the sun itself if need be
to dance in our remembered freedom;
for faith, they say, moves mountains.

Debjani Chatterjee

Mountains once had wings, according to Indian myths.

They're Out There

The ghosts of old dragons
Drift over this town,
Their wings grown as thin
As a princess's gown,
Their scaly skin leaf-like
And wintery brown.

The ghosts of old dragons
Are flitting round town.
Their names are lost treasure,
Each glittering noun
Thrown deep in time's ocean
Where memories drown.

The ghosts of old dragons
Keep haunting this town,
Though long-gone like gas-lamp,
Top-hat and half-crown;
Their presence as false
As the face of a clown.

The ghosts of old dragons
Go growling through town,
As upright as tombstones
Engraved with a frown;
With gravel-path voices
Which wind travels down.

Nick Toczek

The Dragon Who Ate Our School

–1–

The day the dragon came to call,
she ate the gate, the playground wall
and, slate by slate, the roof and all,
the staffroom, gym, and entrance hall,
and every classroom, big or small.

So . . .
She's undeniably great.
She's absolutely cool,
the dragon who ate
the dragon who ate
the dragon who ate our school.

–2–

Pupils panicked. Teachers ran.
She flew at them with wide wingspan.
She slew a few and then began
to chew through the lollipop man,
two parked cars and a Transit van.

Wow . . . !
She's undeniably great.
She's absolutely cool,
the dragon who ate
the dragon who ate
the dragon who ate our school.

–3–

She bit off the head of the head.
She said she was sad he was dead.
He bled and he bled and he bled.
And as she fed, her chin went red
and then she swallowed the cycle shed.

Oh . . .
She's undeniably great.
She's absolutely cool,
the dragon who ate
the dragon who ate
the dragon who ate our school.

–4–

It's thanks to her that we've been freed.
We needn't write. We needn't read.
Me and my mates are all agreed,
we're very pleased with her indeed.
So clear the way, let her proceed.

Cos . . .
She's undeniably great.
She's absolutely cool,
the dragon who ate
the dragon who ate
the dragon who ate our school.

–5–

There was some stuff she couldn't eat.
A monster forced to face defeat,
she spat it out along the street –
the dinner ladies' veg and meat
and that pink muck they serve for sweet.

But . . .
She's undeniably great.
She's absolutely cool,
the dragon who ate
the dragon who ate
the dragon who ate our school.

Nick Toczek

The Dragon in the Cellar

There's a dragon!
There's a dragon!
There's a dragon in the cellar!
Yeah, we've got a cellar-dweller.
There's a dragon in the cellar.

He's a cleanliness fanatic,
takes his trousers and his jacket
to the dragon from the attic
who puts powder by the packet
in a pre-set automatic
with a rattle and a racket
that's disturbing and dramatic.

There's a dragon!
There's a dragon!
There's a dragon in the cellar!
with a flame that's red 'n' yeller.
There's the dragon in the cellar . . .

. . . and a dragon on the roof
who's only partly waterproof,
so she's borrowed an umbrella
from the dragon in the cellar.

There's a dragon!
There's a dragon!
There's a dragon in the cellar!
If you smell a panatella
it's the dragon in the cellar.

And the dragon from the study's
helping out his cellar buddy,
getting wet and soap-suddy
with the dragon from the loo
there to give a hand too,
while the dragon from the porch
supervises with a torch.
Though the dragon from the landing,
through a slight misunderstanding,
is busy paint-stripping and sanding.

There's a dragon!
There's a dragon!
There's a dragon in the cellar!
Find my dad, and tell the feller
there's a dragon in the cellar . . .

. . . where the dragon from my room
goes zoom, zoom, zoom
in a cloud of polish and spray-perfume,
cos he's the dragon whom
they pay to brighten up the gloom
with a mop and a duster and a broom, broom, broom.

There's a dragon!
There's a dragon!
There's a dragon in the cellar!
Gonna get my mum and tell her
there's a dragon in the cellar.

Nick Toczek

Miss King's Kong

It was our 'Bring your pet to school' day . . .

Warren's wolfhound was chasing Paula's poodle
Paula's poodle was chasing Colin's cat
Colin's cat was chasing Harriet's hamster
And Harriet's hamster was chasing Benny's beetle.

Suzie's snake was trying to swallow
Freddie's frog, Percy's parrot, Rebecca's rabbit,
Belinda's bat, Gordon's goat, Peter's pig
And part of Patricia's pony

When all of a sudden everything stopped.

Miss King had brought her pet to school as well.
Miss King's Kong stood there, roared and beat his chest.

Miss King smiled.
Miss King's Kong smiled too
As he swung from the light, eating bananas.

Everything was quiet
Until the Headmaster came in with his pet . . .

Mr Lock's Ness was a real monster.

Paul Cookson

How to Turn a Class Hamster into a Dinosaur

First, prepare your hamster
for life as a ferocious, school-eating dinosaur.
Show it pictures of what life was like
when dinosaurs roamed the earth.
(Ask a teacher.)
Next, motivate it.
Give it lessons on how to scare teachers.
(Diagrams may help.)
Get some prehistoric gooey stuff,
from places unexplored in millions of years . . .
(if your brother has his own room,
it is always a good idea to start looking there).
Smear this gunk on the walls
of the school you want chomped
whilst chanting:
Teachers run and scream and stumble
make a tasty red brick crumble!
Make a giant dino gangsta!
Megasaurus Biggus Hampsta!
Repeat until satisfied.
You now have your very own
Turbosaurus Hamster-beast.

Feed Carefully.

Matt Lees

Good for Discipline

Our teacher's got a dinosaur:
She keeps him in her bottom drawer;
He can't get out, he knows the score
– But, as the silent minutes pass,
You'll hear his muffled dino-roar!

She's shrunk him down to mini-size,
With mini-scales and mini-eyes,
With scary patterns on his thighs
And mini-teeth like spikes of glass,
To bite and tear and terrorise!

She feeds him desks and cloakroom hooks,
She feeds him mice and bats and rooks,
She feeds him smiles and dirty looks,
She feeds him lumps of iron and brass
– And children who forget their books!

His nature's red in tooth and claw,
With powerful legs and crushing jaw;
His belly drags upon the floor
– And if you muck about in class,
You'll meet our teacher's dinosaur!

Tony Charles

Escape Plan

As I, Stegosaurus,
stand motionless
in the museum
I am secretly planning
My escape.

At noon
Tyrannosaurus Rex
will cause a diversion
by wheeling around the museum's high ceilings
and diving at the curators and museum staff
while I
quietly slip out of the fire exit
and melt
into the London crowds.

Roger Stevens

Last Waltz

Solo was a Dodo
the last one in the land.
She didn't go to parties
or dance to birdland bands.
She hadn't got a partner,
she hadn't got a friend,
until –
   she met a Panda,
   a Pandaman called Ben.

Will you dance with me? asked Solo
Can we be a party pair?
Will you take a sprig of blossom
   – will you weave it in my hair?
Will you hold me very tightly?
   – can I hold you to my breast?
   – can I snuggle really closely
      upon your hairy chest?

The woodland flutes played softly,
the evening sang its charms
   to a Panda dancing slowly
     with a Dodo
     in its arms.

Peter Dixon

Dead As a Dodo

They say what starts well ends well,
But for the dodo on Mauritius,
End it sadly diddid
For its start was inauspicious;
Unable to fly it was bound to die
(Did they eat it? And was it delicious?)
How sad to think it's now extinct
A no-no on Mauritius!

Celia Warren

The flightless, defenceless dodos were killed off by 1681.

Dodos

Where did all the dodos go?
That's something only dodos know,
But finding out's no easy task.
There are no dodos left to ask.

Rosie Kent

Mammoth Tasks, Or –
Why the Mammoth Became Extinct

Eat grass.
Eat more grass.
Rub tusks on tree trunk.
Eat grass.

Make huge hairy trumpeting noise
With my lovely mammoth trunk –
Attract beautiful lady mammoth
Make mammoth music together,
Make baby mammoths,
So that mammoth kind will never vanish from the earth . . .
Later.

Right now
Eat grass.

Jan Dean

E

Elements, Seasons and the Natural World

Trees on Parade

The trees are on fire! The trees are on fire!
Call for the fire brigade!
The branches are blazing, the canopies flaming
All along the colonnade.
The trees are on fire, the trees are on fire,
That's the end of the trees, I'm afraid.

Don't worry, they're not burning,
It's just the leaves turning,
In time for their autumn parade.

The trees are all sparkling! The trees are all sparkling!
The sweet chestnut, the aspen and lime
Are laced with fine threads, and delicate beads
Of silver and diamonds and I'm
More or less certain, that gossamer curtain's
Made by crafstmen who worked overtime.

Oh, it's the rime and the dew
On the chestnut and yew,
Those jewels are not worth a dime.

The trees are all dressed up, the trees are all dressed up,
It's a most peculiar thing,
In bright green and pink, the cherry trees, I think,
Are preparing to go to a wedding,
Is that music I hear, from the boughs of the pear,
Have you heard of trees that could sing?

Those are buds and leaves waking,
And birds merry-making,
It always happens in spring.

The trees are in trouble, the trees are in trouble,
They're covered with small coloured balls,
Orange and green, russet and tangerine,
That old tree down by the stone wall
And the one by the road, are bending under their load,
I don't think they look happy at all.

Those are fruit on the boughs,
If you chase off those cows
I can climb up and fill this holdall.

Valerie Bloom

One Moment in Summer

The house is dropping swallows
one by one from under the gutter

they swoop and fall
on our heads as we queue
for ice cream.

It is so hot
that the long line of cars clogging the road
hums like a line of electric fires.

They shine and shimmer, stink of oil and warm seats
the children gaze out from their misted windows.

Trapped under glass
hair plastered down with sweat
gasping for breath like frogs under ice.

The cars crawl round the curve
of the road, stuck in between the shop
and the café.

My ice cream is butterscotch and almond
Lizzie's is chocolate, Harriet's vanilla.

They are so delicious and cold
we lick them slowly, letting the long, cool flavours
slide down our tongues.

Inside the cars, the red-faced people
begin to boil.

The swallows flit and dart
rapid specks of blue, black and white
the summer flies at us
like an arrow.

David Harmer

Summer Farm

The mud cakes dry in the farmyard
The clouds have died a death
The lane shimmers like water
The air is holding its breath.

The dogs fall asleep to the music
Of cruising bumble bees
And the cows stand still as statues
As the stream slides past their knees.

Gareth Owen

one fly everywhere the heat

One fly everywhere the heat

Marlene Mountain

Summery

I love these pure white summer clouds
That drift across blue skies,
The knock-out scent of meadowsweet,
Willows full of sighs
When a breeze goes tickling branches,
And a lark decides to rise.

I love lying in long grasses
Which insects scuffle among,
Where bees helicopter over flowers,
And a stream glug-glugs along,
The lark above right out of sight
But cramming the sky with song.

This is the time for picnics,
Cherry-cake and tea
Poured hot from stubby vacuum flasks,
Plates balanced on your knee,
With cheese and brown-sauce sandwiches,
In the shade of a sycamore tree.

Matt Simpson

River

boat-carrier
bark-lapper
home-provider
tree-reflector
leaf-catcher
field-wanderer
stone-smoother
fast-mover
gentle-stroller
sun-sparkler
sea-seeker

June Crebbin

The Day That Summer Died

From all around the mourners came
   The day that Summer died,
From hill and valley, field and wood
   And lake and mountainside.

They did not come in funeral black
   But every mourner chose
Gorgeous colours or soft shades
   Of russet, yellow, rose.

Horse chestnut, oak and sycamore
   Wore robes of gold and red;
The rowan sported scarlet beads;
   No bitter tears were shed;

Although at dusk the mourners heard,
   As a small wind softly sighed,
A touch of sadness in the air
   The day that Summer died.

Vernon Scannell

Autumn Gilt

The late September sunshine,
Lime green on the linden leaves,
Burns bronze on the slated roof-tops,
Yellow on the farmer's last sheaves.

It flares flame-like on the fire hydrant,
Is ebony on the blackbird's wing,
Blue beryl on the face of the ocean,
Glints gold on the bride's wedding ring.

A sparkling rainbow on the stained-glass window,
It's silver sheen on the kitchen sink,
The late September sunshine
Is a chameleon, I think.

Valerie Bloom

Autumn

Season of conkers and fireworks
and mellow fruitfulness. New shoes,
and a coat that's a bit too big,
to grow into next year. Blackberries
along the canal, white jungles
of frost on the window. Leaves
to kick all the way home,
the smell of bonfires,
stamping the ice on puddles
into crazy paving. The nights come in
early, and you can't play out
after school. Soon
there'll be tangerines in the shops,
in shiny paper like Christmas lights.

The little ones write letters to Santa Claus.

The big ones laugh under the streetlights.

Adrian Henri

Early Winter Diary Poem

18 November 1999

Six-thirty;
   winter dawn –

scraping a thin skin
   of frost
from the windscreen –
   numb fingers fumble –
even the spray
   freezes.
The breeze is
   bitter –
It's so cold
   that stones crack –
that wool freezes
   on the sheep's back.

The birds are too still –
   even the sun
turns its back
   on the day;
but lazy wood-smoke
   idles
over Minchin's roof.

Pie Corbett

Icy Fingers

Despite the cold
A line of old trees
Playing with the moon

Tossing it
From one to the other
Never missing a catch.

Roger McGough

midnight streetlights

midnight streetlights
frost glistens
a road of stars

Pie Corbett

Tanka

Last night, the full moon
hung like a papery lamp
over my quiet road.
I savoured the chilly sky –
the moon tagging my shadow.

Katherine Gallagher

We are a crystal zoo

We are a crystal zoo,
Wielders of fortunes,
The top of our professions.
Like hard silver nails
Hammered into the dark
We make charts for mariners.

John Cotton

The Mysterious Employment of God

To each and every blade of grass,
Apply a coat of whitest gloss.
Brush the trees (on one side)
Soften hills, far and wide.
Solder horizon, cloud and sky,
Make the join invisible to eye.
Windows, wipe with flakes of frost,
Teach smoke to drift, pretend it's lost.
Dress the hedge with spider thread,
Turn to statues flowerbed.
Icicles hang at edge of stream,
Allow the hidden buds to dream.

Andrew Fusek Peters

Thaw

The white garden
softens to green again
and cries silently.

Fred Sedgwick

Spring Magic!

What a fearless magician is Spring –
you really can't teach her a thing!
In she sneaks on a breeze,
draws the leaves from their trees . . .
just when Winter thought *he* was still King!

Judith Nicholls

Winter, Goodbye

Goodbye, Winter.
Adios, snow and ice.
Farewell roaring fires
And wine laced with spice.

Goodbye, frozen fingers.
Goodbye, frozen earth.
Welcome, hints of plenty.
Au revoir, dearth.

Branches now are budding.
Crocuses are up,
Daffodil and snowdrop,
Daisy and buttercup.

Birds have started nesting.
The garden wall is mossed.
Get going, Winter,
And take your frost.

Take your frost with you.
Get on your way.
We welcomed you awhile,
But not today!

It's time you were going.
Your job is done.
Dandelions are lifting
Their heads to the sun.

The year is rested now.
Can't you feel the itch?
There's blossom on the trees,
Spawn in the ditch.

Winter, Goodbye.
It's March now. Remember?
Hit the road, old friend.
See you in December.

Gerard Benson

Spring Assembly

Right! As you all know,
It's spring pretty soon
And I want a real good one this year.
I want no slackers. I want SPRING!
That's S – P – R – I – N – G! Got it?
Spring! Jump! Leap!
Energy! Busting out all over!
Nothing so beautiful! Ding-a-ding-a-ding!

Flowers: I want a grand show from you –
Lots of colours, lots of loveliness.
Daffodils: blow those gold trumpets.
Crocuses: poke up all over the parks and gardens,
Yellows, purples, whites; paint that picture.
And a nice show of blossom on the fruit trees.
Make it look like snow, just for a laugh,
Or loads of pink candy floss.

Winds: blow things about a bit.
North, South, East, West, get it all stirred up
Get March nice and airy and exciting.

Rain: lots of shimmering showers please.
Soak the earth after its winter rest.
Water those seeds and seedlings.
And seeds: start pushing up.
Up! Up! Up! Let's see plenty of green.

Sunshine! Give the earth a sparkle
After the rain. Warm things up.

And you birds: I haven't forgotten you.
Fill the gardens with song.
Build your nests (you'll remember how).
And you lambs: set an example,
Jump, leap, bound, bounce, spring!

And kids: ditch those coats and scarves,
And get running and skipping.
Use that playground, none of this
Hanging about by the school wall
With your hands in your jeans pockets.
It's spring, I tell you.
And you're part of it
And we've got to have a real good one this year.

Gerard Benson

The Day the Sun Got Stuck

It was the day, the night,
the sun got stuck in rising.

In the dark, it prised apart the seam between the earth and
    sky,
like opening a walnut,
eased its fingers through the crack of light,
pushing up the black blind
for the day –
when the earth woke up.

Eyes still shut, earth yawned:
a chill of night went rushing
round hunched hill tops
skidding through a shivering lake
quivering curtains by open windows
winnowing scraps of litter
flapping a sleepy flag
flittering a cat flap
scattering cats to run with tails as big as bulrushes.

And the sun gasped like magma meeting the sea,
feeling the thrill of cold
trickle along its hot, gold fingers.

The milkman and the paperboy look up.
The farmer sensed a missed beat dash like a rat through
   straw,
and, for a second, nothing moved.
Houses stayed asleep in the dark blue streets.
Newspapers shushed the headlines.
Trees froze in their slow sap growing.
A cockerel raised his brown wings, paused, subsided.
Striped bees stayed hived.
A baby held surprise in his new fist,

and then, he cried,
just as the first blackbird,
daybird, nightbird, lifted its head to sing.

Judith Green

F

Friends and
Families

Driving Home

Coming back home from Granny's in the car
I try to stay awake. I really do.
I look around to find the evening star
And make a wish. Who knows? It might come true.

I watch the yellow windows whizzing by
And sometimes see a person in a room,
Cutting a loaf of bread, tying a tie,
Stretching, or watching the telly in the gloom.

I see the street lamps flash past, one by one,
And watch how people's shadows grow and shrink.
It's like a trick; I wonder how it's done
I breathe, and watch, and settle back to think.

But everything gets mixed and far away;
I feel I'm moving but don't know where.
I hear a distant voice which seems to say,
'Wake up! (She's fast asleep.) Wake up! We're there!'

Gerard Benson

Grandad's Garden

is heady with perfumes
wallflowers, carnations,
velvet roses, lilac.

All the bees get tipsy.

He wins prizes. There are
cups, shields around the clock
on the sideboard.

Grandma polishes them
with yellow dusters.

Grandad shows his garden to me
every Sunday. Sweet peas
like bright butterflies,
sky-blue scabious,
the fairy hats of columbines.

His garden is a place
(listen to those ring-a-ding
Canterbury bells!)
that's telling you

what wonderful things
love can do.

Matt Simpson

Sharp Freckles

(for Ben Simmons)

He picks me up, his big thumbs under my armpits tickle,
then puts me down. On his belt there is a shining silver
  buckle.
I hold his hand and see, close up, the dark hairs on his
  knuckles.

He sings to me. His voice is loud and funny and I giggle.
Now we will eat. I listen to my breakfast as it crackles.
He nods and smiles. His eyes are birds in little nests of
  wrinkles.

We kick a ball, red and white, between us. When he tackles
I'm on the ground, breathing a world of grass. It prickles.
He bends. He lifts me high above his head. Frightened, I
  wriggle.

Face to his face, I watch the sweat above each caterpillar
  eyebrow trickle.
He rubs his nose on mine, once, twice, three times, and we
  both chuckle.
He hasn't shaved today. He kisses me. He has sharp
  freckles.

Carol Ann Duffy

In Praise of Aunties

An aunt
is a tender plant.
You really can't
be too fond of an aunt.

Judith Nicholls

Lullaby

If I could write some music for the rain
To play upon your nursery window pane
You'd sleep the sounder for its lullaby
And it would sing more tunefully than I.

If I could teach the clock to tell you tales
Of unicorns and ships with silver sails
You'd never hear the story fail and die
For clocks don't tend to nod as much as I.

If I could knit the shadows into shawls,
Unpick bad dreams and wind them into balls,
We'd throw them through the window at the sky,
Then pull the darkness round us, you and I.

Sue Cowling

Mums

Lovely mums
Cuddly mums
Mums-who-are-chums mums
Small mums
Petite mums
Mums-with-big-bums mums
Silly mums
Daft mums
Dumber-than-dumb mums
Bright mums
Clever mums
Help-you-with-your-sums mums
Neat mums
Fussy mums
Lick-this-and-wipe mums
Misery mums
Glum mums
Mums in the doldrums
Happy mums
Humming mums
Tiddly-um-pum-pum mums
Posh mums
Rich mums
Mouths-full-of-plums mums
Poor mums
Ragged mums
Mums-in-the-slums mums
Brave mums

Humble mums
Take-it-as-it-comes mums
Colourful mums
Flowery mums
Pretty like chrysanthemums
Upright mums
Forthright mums
Crumbs! Mum's-won-a-medal mums
Tumble mums
Fumble mums
Miss nail, hit thumbs, mums
Shirking mums
Working mums
Busy-bumble-bee mums
But for all us daughters
And for all us sons
All the mums in the world
Are the number one mums.

Roger Stevens

Don't Get Your Knickers in a Twist!

We never knew that Mum could be a great contortionist
Until the underwear she wore decided to resist
She aimed straight for the legholes but somehow they
  missed . . .
In a spot the day she got her knickers in a twist.

They restricted and constricted her like an iron fist
Held hostage by the tightening elastic terrorist
One leg round her head and the other round her wrist . . .
A human knot the day she got her knickers in a twist.

She struggled, strained and wrestled but they would not
  desist
The wrangling and the strangling continued to persist
Walking like an alien exhibitionist
A hop, a squat, a trot, she's got her knickers in a twist.

Trussed up like a chicken, peering through her legs she
  hissed,
'Help me quick! What I need's a physiotherapist.'
Dad's reply was casual and utterly dismissed . . .
When he said, 'Do not fret
There's no need to panic yet
Play it cool, just don't get your knickers in a twist.'

Paul Cookson

Shell

Said a mother crab to her daughter,
'Look, that's Brighton Pier,
So pick up that shell my darling
And tell me what you hear.'

The babe picked up the shining shell
Off the gritty sand
And placing it carefully to her ear said,
'I can hear the land.'

Gareth Owen

'Goodbye'

Daddy was a magician –
made things happen when he
appeared at random weekends.

Spurring us into action
like kittens serving at table
in the Museum of Curiosities at Bramber.

Visiting: castles, museums, and Nelson's ship;
Victory – safely harboured –
history for the price of a ticket.

Stirring the rain at Butlins
riding the *Merry Mixer*
while everyone else took shelter.

Spinning a gyroscope on his hand
level at every angle and turn
in *The Ideal Home Exhibition*.

Watching cine-films of Deputy Dawg
whirring on our sitting room wall,
a cartoon desert highway in Seafield Road.

Fizz; click; whirr, but –
no time to say the magic word
before he disappeared.

Janina Aza Karpinska

Sisters

Sally hasn't talked to me for ages.
    She shouts, she swears
    She sneers and jeers, she rages
    She stamps around and slams the door
But doesn't *talk*.
All she'll say to me these days is
'Get lost, go away,
Leave me *alone!*'

Sally hasn't laughed with me for ages.
    She doesn't smile
    Or grin or giggle,
    Won't share a joke.
And when I tell her something funny
She throws her eyes up to the ceiling
Says, as if to someone else:
'Why don't that stupid kid shut up!'

Sally hasn't played with me for ages.
    We used to get the doll's house out,
    Go skipping in the street, or
    To the playground in the park together.
But now, it's like it never happened,
She's trying to pretend
Even to me
She's never *played* with anything, not never.

Sally hasn't wanted me for ages.
  She's getting too *grown-up*
  To be seen with me,
  She reckons.
But I can get my own back, don't you worry.
It's nearly bedtime and I've hidden
The teddy bear
She sleeps with every night.

(And in a little while we'll see
How grown-up my sister Sally
Really is . . .)

Mick Gowar

Listn Big Brodda Dread, Na!

My sista is younga than me.
My sista outsmart five-foot three.
My sista is own car repairer
and yu nah catch me doin judo with her.

   I sey I wohn get a complex
   I wohn get a complex.
   Then I see the muscles my sista flex.

My sista is tops at disco dance.
My sista is well into self-reliance.
My sista plays guitar and drums
and wahn see her knock back double rums.

   I sey I wohn get a complex
   I wohn get a complex.
   Then I see the muscles my sista flex.

My sista doesn mind smears of grease and dirt.
My sista'll reduce yu with sheer muscle hurt.
My sista says no guy goin keep her phone-bound –
with own car my sista is a wheel-hound.

   I sey I wohn get a complex
   I wohn get a complex.
   Then I see the muscles my sista flex.

James Berry

Megan's Day

Like any day
I open our front door.
Against the creosote fence,
Above the clustering pansies
The roses glow dull red,
And further off
Beyond the maple
And the overgrown canal
The orphan hill
That has no name
Rises to the blue.

Brakes squeal.
Ann, the driver, wears a boiler suit
And works at Revill's garage in the town.
'Remind your mum
To leave me half a dozen eggs,'
She shouts, her eyes upon the road ahead.

Because it's June and hot today
I sit with Kelly at the back
Beside an open window.
She's not my best friend
But you can always talk to her.
The wind that's blown across the Irish Sea
And half the breadth of Wales
Before rustling our homework books
And my brown hair
Smells hot this day of grass and tar.

Today we're up to Air and Light
In our Jam Jar Science Books.
Later we'll climb on the roof
To drop paper parachutes
On to the playing fields below.
Around the iron gates
The children shout and stare
As we get off the bus.
Next September I'll be at the High School
And someone else
Will sit in my place by the window.
There are stars that die each minute
Before their light comes down to us.
The bell rings
And we crowd shouting
Towards the shadows and the open door.

Gareth Owen

Singing with Recordings

We lick same stick of ice cream.
We tickle each other to screams.

Just as each catches the ball from each
we leap the other's back with a touch.

Knowing each one's hating and loving
we rush with whispers to our hiding.

We get buried in the sand together.
We sing with recordings together.

We blow that one lucky-dip whistle.
We share our one used-tissue.

Not unlike two head-to-tail horses
there, standing in the rain
we get showered together again and again.

James Berry

Betrayal

Like rollerblades, we make a pair.
Watch us practise; with such flair
Pavements fly beneath our feet
In this kingdom of concrete
The original polyurethane pals
Surfing down suburban hills
Gossip, giggle, God it's great
To hang out with my best mate.

But my best mate's become a spy,
Sold my secrets. I blink my eye
And he has gone to the other side.
The Gang ride by; I try to hide,
Cover my feelings with concrete
As pavements fly beneath my feet
I climb the hills of hurt and hate
To get away from my best mate.

Andrew Fusek Peters

Fantasy Christmas List

The thing
about going round
to Robert Baker's house
is that something that little bit different
would happen
every time

For instance
one Saturday afternoon
in May
we were up in Robert's bedroom
and I said 'So what shall we do?'
and Robert said 'A fantasy Christmas list, of course.'
And I said 'Why not?'

When we'd finished
Robert showed me
his list of things:

    A very fast red sports car
    A house in America with a swimming pool
    A day at the BBC
    A naked lady
    A baby armadillo
    A real magic wand

And then I showed Robert my list of things:

A giant conker
A massive box of cheese and onion crisps
A new trainspotting annual
A huge bottle of cream soda
A naked lady

Then Robert
got in a right old huff
said 'You copied
    my naked lady,
    didn't you?'
and made me
cross it off my list

James Carter

G

Girls' Stuff

What are Little Girls Made of?

What are little girls made of, made of?
What are little girls made of?
　Sugar and spice
　And all things nice,
That's what little girls are made of.

Anon.

Mermaid School

(A crowd of little fishes is called a school.
So what is a crowd of little mermaids
called? Perhaps it is a SPLASH!)

What do mermaids learn at school?

How to sing beside a pool.
How to catch a flying fish.
How to grant an earth-child's wish.
How to chime a ship's old bell.
How to curl inside a shell.
How to win a sea-horse race.
How to swoop and dive and chase
Faster than the dolphin teams.

How to swim the silver beams
Of the small and misty moon.
How to play a magic tune.
How to tame a hungry shark.
How to find (when nights grow dark)
Hidden caves where treasures lie.
How to read a cloudy sky.
How to make a pearly ring.
How to mend a seabird's wing.
How to use a golden comb.
How to balance on the foam.
How to greet a friendly whale.
How to spin upon your tail.
How to twist and leap and turn . . .

This is what the mermaids learn.

Clare Bevan

Best Friends

It's Susan I talk to not Tracey,
Before that I sat next to Jane;
I used to be best friends with Lynda
But these days I think she's a pain.

Natasha's all right in small doses,
I meet Mandy sometimes in town;
I'm jealous of Annabel's pony
And I don't like Nicola's frown.

I used to go skating with Catherine,
Before that I went there with Ruth;
And Kate's so much better at trampoline
She's a show-off, to tell you the truth.

I think that I'm going off Susan,
She borrowed my comb yesterday;
I think I might sit next to Tracey,
She's my nearly best friend: she's OK.

Adrian Henri

Silverly

Silverly,
  Silverly
Over the
  Trees
The moon drifts
  By on a
Runaway
  Breeze.
Dozily,
  Dozily,
Deep in her
  Bed,
A little girl
  Dreams with the
Moon in her
  Head.

Dennis Lee

Get Your Things Together, Hayley

Mum said the dreaded words this morning,
'Get your things together, Hayley,
We're moving.'

I've at last made a friend, and Mrs Gray
Has just stopped calling me
The New Girl.

Why do we have to go now
When I'm just beginning
To belong?

It's OK for my sister,
She's good with people.
They like her.

But I can't face the thought
Of starting all over again,
In the wrong uniform,

Knowing the wrong things,
In a class full of strangers
Who've palled up already

And don't need me.
Mum says, 'It's character forming, Hayley.'
I say it's terribly lonely.

Frances Nagle

Girl Footballer

The ball soars and the ball flies.
The ball goes up. The ball goes in.
And the balls in your eyes
are rolling and spinning,
spinning and rolling.
And the blood in your heart is singing.

You feel yourself whirl and twirl.
What a talented girl.
Nothing like this feeling you get
when the ball bulges in the back of the net.
No, you don't easily forget
the sweet sweet taste of a goal.
Replay it in your mind again:

Left foot in the air, flick,
straight to the back of the net.
Play it again and again
– the ball's beautiful roll to the goal.
Nothing like the soaring and roaring
when the plump ball hits the thin net.
And the sad blue goalie sits on the sad green grass.
The look on the slow face,
watching the ball go past, fast.
No chance. No chance. Watching the ball dance.
You dribble from the midfield down.
You get past three men.
You do a chip, a volley, you curl the ball.

You perm the air with your talent, and all
the fans sizzle and spark,
all the fans sing and dance,
football is one long romance
with the ball, with the ball and all.

You nutmeg the goalie like the goalie is a spice.
You get the ball in, not once, twice, but thrice!
Hat trick! You make the goalie feel sick.
So you lie down and roll in celebration.
You feel the team jump on your back
then you feel the whole nation,
goggle-eyed in admiration.
You squeeze your fist,
like this, like a kiss, to the wild crowd
and your football of a heart is bouncing and proud.

Jackie Kay

No One Can Call Me

Here is my heaven – on the top of a bus.
I gaze down on the no-time world.
People hurry along pavements:
women with shopping-bags and children;
men with brief-cases.
No time to look at one another
because their eyes are on the clock.
No clock to see but they feel it,
feel its hands pulling them along
away from now,
pulling them away from themselves,
making their minds its mainspring.

Here, up a stairway out of time,
I am my real self in a real world.
No one can call me, catch me –
I am not there.
Ideas are stirring underground
pushing up green shoots into the sun –
I'm wrapped in sun in this plate-glass corner.
There are three of us
travelling alone, coming back to ourselves
on the top of a double-decker bus.

Phoebe Hesketh

Treasure Trove

I have a tin
to keep things in
underneath
my bedroom floor.

I put my finger
in the crack,
quietly lift
the floorboard back,

and there's my store,
safely hid
in a tin with roses
on the lid.

A few feathers
and a chicken's claw,
a big tooth
from a dinosaur,

the wrapper
from my Easter Egg,
a Christmas robin
with one leg,

long hairs
from a horse's mane,
real pesetas
come from Spain,

three of my
operation stitches,
like spiders
wrapped in bandages,

a marble
full of dragon smoke,
flashing with fire
in the dark,

a magic pebble
round and white,
a sparkler left
from bonfire night.

Underneath
my bedroom floor
there's a treasure tin,
with my things in.

Irene Rawnsley

Gillian Costigan

I wish I was Gillian Costigan,
with hair brushed sleek
and clothes that fit.
I wish I was Gillian Costigan
with money in my pocket every single week.

Her smile is wide,
her shoes have a shine,
she has friends to tea,
she laughs all the time.

I wish I was Gillian Costigan.
She has holidays in Greece,
her Dad loves her Mum,
she has nieces and nephews,
a Nan *and* a Gran,
her sarnies are thick
with hard cheese *and* ham.

I wish I was Gillian Costigan
with a slide in my hair,
a huge Mum to hug me,
a new top to wear.

Chrissie Gittins

Chocoholic

Into the half-pound box of Moonlight
my small hand crept.
There was an electrifying rustle.
There was a dark and glamorous scent.
Into my open, moist mouth
the first Montelimar went.

Down in the crinkly second layer,
five finger-piglets snuffled
among the Hazelnut Whirl,
the Caramel Square,
the Black Cherry and Almond Truffle.

Bliss.

I chomped. I gorged.
I stuffed my face,
till only the Coffee Cream
was left for the owner of the box –
tough luck, Anne Pope –
oh, and half an Orange Supreme.

Carol Ann Duffy

We Are the Year Six Girls

We are the Year Six Girls
We are the Year Six Crowd
We are the Year Six Posse
We are the Girls Out Loud

We are the Year Six Sisters
And we know how to have a laugh
We scare the Year Six boys for sure
And they don't dare cross our path

The teachers say we're a dream to teach
But they haven't got a clue
In lessons we're quiet and well behaved
If only the teachers knew

That we're passing notes and swapping jokes
And discussing various ploys
To humiliate and aggravate
And generally wind up the boys

We are the Year Six Girls
What else did you expect?
We are the Year Six Posse
So treat us with respect.

Roger Stevens

There Was a Little Girl

There was a little girl
Who had a little curl
Right in the middle of her forehead.
When she was good
She was very, very good,
But when she was bad she was horrid.

Henry Wadsworth Longfellow

Fairy Picnic

Under our kitchen table
on the new carpet
the fairies have prepared a picnic –
Tiny little cookies,
funny little flakes
weeny little biscuits,
scrummy fairy cakes . . .
sarnies small as bee eyes,
pretty little buns.
It's called a fairy picnic . . .

But my mum
says
they're just crumbs!

Peter Dixon

The Choosy Princess

(Clare found this poem in a robin's nest.)

The Choosy Princess wanted only the best,
So she set all her Princes a puzzling quest . . .

'You must find me the bird
With invisible wings,
The spear of a flower,
The time-telling rings,
And the bright, golden kingdom
Without any kings.'

The Princes rode off down the long, winding track,
But none of them, none of them, ever came back.

The Choosy Princess took her crown from the shelf.
'If the task is so tricky, I'll try it myself.'

I'll search for the bird
With invisible wings,
The spear of a flower,
The time-telling rings,
And the bright, golden kingdom
Without any kings.'

She strolled round the lawns with the gardener's son,
They looked for her treasures and found EVERY one.

'My puzzle was simple. The task was quite small,'
She laughed as she happily counted them all.

'Here's the egg of a songbird,
(With no wings to see!)
The thorn of a rosebush
The rings of a tree,
And a sweet, golden comb
From the hive of a bee.'

Then she married the boy she had loved all along –
The gardener's boy, who was clever and strong.

Clare Bevan

Little Miss Muffet

Little Miss Muffet
sat on her tuffet
eating her butties with Bert.

A spider crawled on her hand:
she picked it up and
shoved it straight down the back of his shirt.

Dave Calder

When I Grow up and Have Children

When I grow up and have children,
And they ask if they can use the phone,
I'll tell them, 'You can't, if you want to call someone
You'll have to buy a phone of your own.'

When I grow up and have children,
And they ask if they can stay up late,
I'll say, 'You can't, even if you're eighteen,
You must be asleep by eight.'

When I grow up and have children,
And they ask if they can play in the street,
I'll say, 'No, you can't, what more do you want,
We've the backyard, that square of concrete.'

And when my children get angry and cry,
I'll ask them, 'What can I do?
I learnt everything I know from my Mum,'
That's right, I'll blame it on you.

Valerie Bloom

Counting Rhyme for a Young Princess

*(Clare found this rhyme under a bundle of
royal arithmetic books.)*

12 Naughty girls, dancing on their toes.
11 Wild swans, white as winter snows.
10 Beds of feathers for a REAL princess.
 9 Silver buttons on a golden dress.
 8 Tiny mice, stitching tiny stitches.
 7 Kindly dwarfs, sharing all their riches.
 6 Lonely years in Rapunzel's tower.
 5 Witch's fingers, full of wicked power.
 4 Twisty pathways (one will lead to glory).
 3 Magic wishes in a bedtime story.
 2 Ugly sisters, angry and alarming.
 1 Little slipper and one Prince Charming.

Clare Bevan

H

Home Life

I Remember, I Remember

I remember, I remember,
The house where I was born,
The little window where the sun
Came peeping in at morn;
He never came a wink too soon,
Nor brought too long a day,
But now, I often wish the night
Had borne my breath away!

I remember, I remember,
The roses, red and white,
The violets, and the lily-cups,
Those flowers made of light!
The lilacs where the robin built,
And where my brother set
The laburnum on his birth-day, –
The tree is living yet!

I remember, I remember,
Where I was used to swing.
And thought the air must rush as fresh
To swallows on the wing;
My spirit flew in feathers then,
That is so heavy now,
And summer pools could hardly cool
The fever on my brow!

I remember, I remember,
The fir trees dark and high;
I used to think their slender tops
Were close against the sky;
It was a childish ignorance,
But now 'tis little joy
To know I'm farther off from heaven
Than when I was a boy.

Thomas Hood

At Cider Mill Farm

I remember my uncle's farm
Still in midsummer
Heat hazing the air above the red rooftops
Some cattle sheds, a couple of stables
Clustered round a small yard
Lying under the hills that stretched their long back
Through three counties.

I rolled with his dogs
Among the straw bales
Stacked high in the barn he built himself
During a storm one autumn evening
Tunnelled for treasure or jumped with a scream
From a pirate ship's mast in the straw
Burrowed for gold and found he'd buried
Three battered Ford cars deep in the hay.

He drove an old tractor that sweated oil
In long black streaks down rusty orange
It chugged and whirred, coughed into life
Each day as he clattered across the cattle grids
I remember one night my cousin and I
Dragging back cows from over the common
We prodded the giant steaming flanks
Pushed them homeward through the rain
And then drank tea from huge tin mugs
Feeling like farmers.

He's gone now, he sold it
But I have been back for one last look
To the twist in the lane that borders the stream
Where Mary, Ruth and I once waded
Water sloshing over our wellies
And I showed my own children my uncle's farm
The barn still leaning over the straw
With for all I know, three battered Ford cars
Still buried beneath it.

David Harmer

Tanka

A letter from home
wafts in the smell of sand
in the monsoon rains –
dusk falls and I hear the peal
of temple bells in the wind . . .

Usha Kishore

My Mum's Speedy Day

My mum
Leaps out of bed,
Flips through the paper,
Flies round with the vacuum,

Dashes off a letter,
Nips to the loo,
Pops to the shops,

Runs slap bang into friends,
Races home,
Grabs a bite to eat,

Flicks through the TV channels,
Snatches forty winks,
Leaps out of bed . . .

John Coldwell

Dear Mum

While you were out
A cup went and broke itself on purpose.
A crack appeared in that old blue vase your great granddad
Got from Mr Ming.
Somehow without me even turning on the tap
The sink mysteriously overflowed.
A strange jam-stain, about the size of my hand,
Suddenly appeared on the kitchen wall.
I don't think we'll ever discover exactly how the cat
Managed to turn on the washing machine
(Specially from the inside)
Or how Sis's pet rabbit went and mistook
The waste-disposal unit for a burrow.
I can tell you, I was really scared when, as if by magic,
A series of muddy footprints appeared on your new white
    carpet.
Also, I know the canary looks grubby,
But it took ages and ages
Getting it out of the vacuum-cleaner
I was being good (honest)
But I think the house is haunted so,
Knowing you're going to have a fit,
I've gone over to Gran's to lie low for a bit.

Brian Patten

Message on the Table

Your dinner is in the
Oven because I'm taking
Uncle
Jack
Up to your grandmother's.
She hasn't seen him in years.
There's also extra sauce in
A pan on the stove. It needs
To be warmed through
Even if you manage to get in on time.
Wash up and
Open a can of something if you're still
Really hungry, although you
May not be if you work out my
Secret.

David Kitchen

Crazy Mayonnaisy Mum

When my friends come home with me
They never want to stay for tea
Because of Mum's peculiar meals
Like strawberries with jellied eels.
You should see her lick her lips
And sprinkle sugar on the chips,
Then pass a cup of tea to you
And ask, 'One salt or two?'

Whoops-a-daisy
That's my crazy
Mayonnaisy mum.

She serves up ice cream with baked beans,
And golden syrup with sardines,
And curried chocolate mousse on toast,
And once she iced the Sunday roast.
When my birthday comes she'll make
A steak and kidney birthday cake.
There'll be jelly too, of course,
With cheese and onion sauce.

Whoops-a-daisy,
That's my crazy
Mayonnaisy mum.

What's she put in my packed lunch?
A bag of rhubarb crisps to crunch.
Lots of sandwiches as well,
But what is in them? Who can tell?
It tastes like marmalade and ham,
Or maybe fish paste mixed with jam.
What's inside my flask today?
Spinach squash – hooray!

Whoops-a-daisy,
That's my crazy
Mayonnaisy mum.

Julia Donaldson

Vac

Our vacuum cleaner
Sucked up the cat
The morning paper
The kitchen mat
Two dozen spiders
A pair of shoes
A vest and panties
(I'm not sure whose)
Some CDs and
Cassettes galore
A nest of tables
The bathroom door
The electric cooker
The TV set
An ancient poster
Of Wet, Wet, Wet
Our neighbour's dog
The postman, too
Our dining chairs
The upstairs loo
Some plastic bricks
And – what a drag!
I think it needs
A change of bag . . .

Trevor Harvey

Santa Claws

I don't know why they're blaming me
When all I did was climb a tree
And bat a shiny silver ball.
How could I know the tree would fall?
And when those silly lights went out
They didn't have to scream and shout
And turf me out and shut the door.
Now no one loves me any more.
I'm in the kitchen by myself
But wait! What's on that high-up shelf?
A lovely turkey, big and fat!
How nice! They *do* still love their cat.

Julia Donaldson

Walking the Dog Seems Like Fun to Me

I said, The dog wants a walk.

Mum said to Dad, It's your turn.
Dad said, I always walk the dog.
Mum said, Well I walked her this morning.
Dad said, She's your dog.
I didn't want a dog in the first place.

Mum said, It's your turn.

Dad stood up and threw the remote control
at the pot plant.
Dad said, I'm going down the pub.
Mum said, Take the dog.

Dad shouted, No way!
Mum shouted, You're going nowhere!
I grabbed Judy's lead
and we both bolted out the back door.

The stars were shining like diamonds.
Judy sniffed at a hedgehog, rolled up in a ball.
She ate a discarded kebab on the pavement.
She tried to chase a cat that ran up a tree.

Walking the dog
seems like fun to me.

Roger Stevens

Perishing

It's down to freezing:
Indoors,
the hunting cat is suddenly tame;
Outside,
late cars
start getting their skates on.

It's five below:
Outside,
windows draw patterns
with broken pencils;
Indoors,
the cat beats us
to the warmest places
and warns us with his eye.

It's ten below:
Indoors,
the cat thrums,
soft
as an oiled engine;
Outside,
puddles
are hardening
their hearts.

David Orme

Feeding the Aardvark

My father says I don't concentrate.

My mother says I get up too late.

My teachers say I'm a nuisance:

it's useless,
because words like *zebra* sleep on my pillow,
perpendicular, codgy –
and when I wake up in the listening dark
I whisper them;
lackadaisical
aardvark
toxic
strop.
The duvet hisses and humps itself,
Doo-vay, I say, hushing it to lullaby.
My cat stretches with a shudder
like a swan settling in bubbles of full-fat milk
then he flies up and sits by my head
tapping the stripes of the zebra
where the street light falls on the sheet.
He's a catowl: clutching a branch of my hair
under his paws, his great feathered face singing.
Silly old codgy, I purr and a noun
bounces off the ceiling.

In the morning my teacher tells me
I'm tiresome;
we meet in the dictionary: *annoying, fatiguing, tedious.*

Tonight, I shall feed *annoying*
to the aardvark – he's not too fussy about his diet,
but I shall put *fatiguing* and *tedious* together
under my pillow to hatch.

Judith Green

The Music I Like

The music I like
Is very special music.

At this moment,
For instance,

I'm listening to the washing machine
Slowing down,

As the gerbil rattles
In its cage,

And my wife runs
Up the stairs

And my next-door neighbour
Cuts his grass.

Music, very special music.
Just listen . . .

Ian McMillan

I

Impossible and Incredible

Changed

For months he taught us, stiff-faced.
His old tweed jacket closely buttoned up,
his gestures careful and deliberate.

We didn't understand what he was teaching us.
It was as if a veil, a gauzy bandage, got between
what he was showing us and what we thought we saw.

He had the air of a gardener, fussily protective
of young seedlings, but we couldn't tell
if he was hiding something or we simply couldn't see it.

At first we noticed there were often scraps of leaves
on the floor where he had stood. Later, thin wisps
of thread like spider's web fell from his jacket.

Finally we grew to understand the work. And on that day
he opened his jacket, which to our surprise
seemed lined with patterned fabric of many shimmering hues.

Then he smiled and sighed. And with this movement
the lining rippled and instantly the room was filled
with a flickering storm of swirling butterflies.

Dave Calder

The Picnic

They biked to the end of the world one day
where the sea tumbled over the brink
and they took out a flask and a couple of cups
and poured themselves something to drink.
They gazed at the waters cascading
in a foaming and terrible wall
and murmured (while spreading a cloth out)
that the world must be flat after all.
They brought out some ketchup and Marmite
as a phoenix erupted in flames
and they ate a cheese sandwich with pickle
before they got up for a game.
A unicorn nibbled their cupcakes
as they dribbled a football around
swatting at minuscule dragons
which flew up in swarms from the ground.
As the sun set in fiery glory
and the sea put it out with a hiss,
they cleared up their rubbish and, yawning,
tossed it into the abyss.
The night sky was blazing with starlight
as the pair of them cycled away.
They arrived home at three in the morning
and were late in for work the next day.

Marian Swinger

At Three in the Morning

When the fairground is silent and empty
And the candyfloss crowds have gone home,
The roundabout horses start dreaming
Of sun-swept sierras to roam,
Of canyons that clatter with hoof-beats,
Of rivers that shatter like glass,
Of galloping, never in circles again,
But straight through the heavens of grass.

Richard Edwards

The Rainmaker Danced

The rainmaker danced
the rainmaker danced
the rainmaker danced.

Down came
the rains
in a flash
and that was the end
of cricket match.

The rainmaker danced
the rainmaker danced
the rainmaker danced.

Sky changed
from blue
to grey
and barbecue
was washed away

'What rotten luck!'
cried everyone, faces grim.
But what can you expect
when the rainmaker
was a magical duck
and dying for a swim.

John Agard

Cold Spell

for Ruth Underhill

'A cold spell,' said the weatherman
and my boiler's on the blink –
no central heating! I've just seen
a walrus in my kitchen sink.

P-p-p-p-penguins (not the chocolate kind)
are waddling down the hall,
whilst polar bears play on the stairs,
throwing giant snowballs.

A reindeer, with bright red nose,
is snoozing in the loo,
together with some Friesian cows
or are they eskimoos?

Two dozen elves fill up my shelves –
they're making too much noise –
wrapping up, then stacking up
gifts for girls and boys.

Yes, Father Christmas has moved
in to 36, The Crescent:
so be good children, my new job
is labelling the presents.

Mike Johnson

The Kleptomaniac

Beware the Kleptomaniac
Who knows not wrong from right
He'll wait until you turn your back
Then steal everything in sight:

The nose from a snowman
(Be it carrot or coal)

The stick from a blind man
From the beggar his bowl

The smoke from a chimney
The leaves from a tree

A kitten's miaow
(Pretty mean you'll agree)

He'll pinch a used tea bag
From out of the pot

A field of potatoes
And scoff the whole lot

(Is baby still there,
Asleep in its cot?)

He'll rob the baton
From a conductor on stage

All the books from the library
Page by page

He'll snaffle your shadow
As you bask in the sun

Pilfer the currants
From out of your bun

He'll lift the wind
Right out of your sails

Hold your hand
And make off with your nails

When he's around
Things just disappear

F nnily eno gh I th nk
Th re's one ar und h re!

Roger McGough

Mary Celeste – High Street,
Monday, 8.32 a.m.

When we found the number 57 bus,
The engine was still running,
But there was no driver
In the cab.
On the top deck
And the bottom deck
There wasn't a single passenger,
Though on one of the seats we discovered
A half-eaten Mars bar.
Everyone seemed to have left
In a hurry,
For we found
Two umbrellas,
Three briefcases,
And a lunch box containing
An apple, a cheese sandwich,
And a packet of Smoky Bacon crisps.

The passengers had
Completely disappeared.
Some people think they were captured by aliens.
Others say a giant squid squirmed out of the drain
And swallowed them whole.
Some blame pirates
From rival bus companies.
Me? I think they all decided
They just couldn't be bothered
To go to work or school
On a wet Monday morning,
So they all grew wings
And flew off into the sky,
Led by the conductor shouting
'Any more fairies?'

David Orme

Grandma Was Eaten by a Shark!

Grandma was eaten by a shark
Dad, by a killer whale
And my baby brother got slurped up
By a rather hungry sea snail.

A cuttlefish cut my mum to bits
An octopus strangled my sister
A jellyfish stung my auntie's toes
Giving her terrible blisters.

A pufferfish poisoned my grandpa
A dogfish ate my cat
And then a catfish ate my dog!
I was very upset about that.

So you go for a swim if you like
Just don't ask me to come too
I'm staying here with my camera
I can't wait to see what gets you!

Andrea Shavick

Disguise

Every morning after I shampoo my fur
I climb into my humanskin costume and
Put on my human mask and human clothes.

Then I go out into the human city
And catch a human bus to work.

As I sit at my computer
Summoning up images of the financial world
None of my colleagues know
That inside my human hand gloves
Are the brown and burly
Sharp and curly
Paws of a grizzly bear.

Yes, I am a bear in cunning disguise,
Only passing as human
Trying not to yield to temptation
As I lumber past
The sticky buns in the baker's shop
The honeycombs in the health shop

I am married to a human woman who knows my secret
We have a human daughter
Who is rather furry and has deep golden eyes
And gentle paws
We call her Bruinhilda

I took Bruinhilda to a circus once
But there was a performing bear
Riding a unicycle, juggling with flames
Dancing to an accordion

I sat tight
Though she might have been my mother
I sat tight
While the inside of my human mask
Filled up with the tears of a bear.

Adrian Mitchell

No Bread

I wish I'd made a list
I forgot to get the bread.
If I forget it again
I'll be dead.

We had blank and butter pudding,
beans on zip.
Boiled egg with deserters,
no chip butty: just chip.

I wish I'd made a list
I forgot to get the bread.
My mam got the empty bread bin
and wrapped it round my head.

Our jam sarnies were just jam
floating on the air.
We spread butter on the table
cos the bread wasn't there.

My mam says if I run away
she knows I won't be missed,
not like the bread was . . .
I wish I'd made a list!

Ian McMillan

The Secret Rhyme for Orange

Where's the secret rhyme for Orange?
Is it lurking somewhere near?
Go and look under the sofa.
No? There's only grey fluff there?

Then where is that stupid rhyme?
I've been looking now for days!
Searching through the dictionary
Is like searching through a maze.

How can a word have no rhyme?
It really is not funny,
Orange is not a lonely word –
It's always seemed quite chummy.

You'd think if a word had no rhyme
It would be one like 'Grim' or 'Bad',
Not a juicy word like Orange –
It really makes me mad.

Look amongst the leaves of the Orange tree.
See if the rhyme's sleeping there
Curled up in the branches
Without a worldly care.

Look in the caverns of the sun,
Look on Jupiter and Mars.
If they've got a rhyme for Orange
Bring it back. It's ours.

Brian Patten

J
Journeys

Days

Days fly by on holidays,
they escape like birds
released from cages.
What a shame you can't buy
tokens of time, save them up
and lengthen the good days,
or maybe you could tear out time
from days that drag, then pay it back
on holidays, wild days,
days you wish would last for ever.
You could wear these days with pride,
fasten them like poppies to your coat,
or keep them in a tin, like sweets,
a confection of days
to be held on the tongue
and tasted, now and then.

Brian Moses

I Love Our Orange Tent

I love our orange tent.
We plant it like a flower in the field.
The grass smells sweet inside it.

And at night
When we're lying in it
I hear the owl crying.

When the wind blows
My tent flaps
Like a huge bird,
Like an orange owl.

And sometimes
I hear the rain
Pattering
Like little dancing feet.
And I feel warm and safe
Inside my tent.

But when the sun shines –!
When I wake up
And the sun is shining
It pours like yellow honey over us.

I love my orange tent.

Berlie Doherty

Figure

When I arrived Suilven
wore a scarf of cloud

across her shoulder.
Next day, pouting at Canisp,

a chestnut beret at half cock.
Her skirts were low

with mist on Thursday.
Today, her shape,

with sun, is kissed.

Chrissie Gittins

Suilven and Canisp are mountains in Sutherland in Scotland.

At Home, Abroad

All summer
I dream of
places I've never
been
where I might
see faces
I've never seen,
like the dark
face of my
father in
Nigeria,
or the pale
face of my
mother in
the Highlands,
or the bright
faces of my
cousins at
Land's end.

All summer
I spell the names
of tricky countries
just in case
I get a sudden
invite: Madagascar,
Cameroon. I draw
cartoons of
airports, big and small.
Who will meet me?
Will they
shake hands or
kiss both cheeks?
I draw
duty frees
with every
country's favourite
sweetie, smiling
a sugary welcome,
and myself,
cap-peaked,
wondering if I am
'home'.

Jackie Kay

Postcard Poem: Solo

Mum, you needn't have worried one bit.
I travelled fine, fine, solo. Carried
in steelbird-belly of music shows.
I ate two passengers' pudding twice.
Nibbled nothings nutty and chocolatey.
Sipped cool Cokes. Had more nibbles.
All over mountain after mountain.
Over different oceans. Over
weird clouds, like snow hills
with trails of straggly shapes
drifting, searching. And strangers
talked – Germans going on big-fish hunt,
Italians to ride glass-bottomed boat,
a Dane to do snorkelling. Then, Mum,
I hopped from steelbird-belly, among
sun-roasted people of a palmtree place.
Welcome to Jamaica, voices called out.
Whole family hugged a sweating me
and took me off. Other exotics
got collected up in cars and coaches
to be naked on beaches, while
steelbird stood there shining-ready
for more come-and-go migrations.

James Berry

Journey Home

I remember the long homeward ride, begun
By the light that slanted in from the level sun;
And on the far embankment, in sunny heat,
Our whole train's shadow travelling, dark and complete.

A farmer snored. Two loud gentlemen spoke
Of the cricket and news. The pink baby awoke
And gurgled awhile. Till slowly out of the day
The last light sank in glimmer and ashy-grey.

I remember it all; and dimly remember, too,
The place where we changed – the dark trains
    lumbering through;
The refreshment-room, the crumbs and the slopped tea;
And the salt on my face, not of tears, not tears,
    but the sea.

Our train at last! Said Father, 'Now tumble in!
It's the last lap home!' And I wondered what 'lap'
    could mean;
But the rest is all lost, for a huge drowsiness crept
Like a yawn upon me; I leant against Mother and slept.

John Walsh

London Underground: Terms and Conditions

Please mind the gap,
Between you and me.

Smiling on this carriage
Is prohibited,
Maximum penalty:
A bemused stare.

Maintenance work may be carried out,
Nail filing,
Combing of hair, et cetera.
Glances are forbidden.

The next station is:
Work
It is unavoidable.
Passengers cannot cross on to another line.

Thank you for not smiling.
Please mind the gap,
Between you and me.

Catriona Burns (aged 12)

The Ascent of Vinicombe

He took his bag off his back and strapped it to his chest.
I think this is the start of an adventure, he declared,
and so it was. With great care we roped ourselves together,
then slowly, cautiously, we fought our way up the ice-cliff.
He led, of course, shouting warnings and encouragement as
  he sprang
from boulder to boulder, dodging avalanches. It was hard
  going.
There was no shelter from the bitter wind and only one
lamp-post strong enough to bear our weight. We paused a
  moment
then pressed on, any delay was dangerous. Without warning
the pavement would split, opening horrid pits, crevasses
crammed with writhing snakes or hairy mammoths.
  Despite it all,
we struggled upwards, risking a traverse of the slippery
  railings,
until we hauled each other, wild-eyed and wind-beaten,
  across the glacier
of Kersland Street. It was then that, with amazing speed,
he slipped his coat off and hung it cape-like from his head,
announced his possession of super-powers and flew, arms
  outstretched,
up the lane towards the school.

Dave Calder

The Cruise of the Bumblebee

'Twas a wild and windy blustery night
When we shipped on the *Bumblebee*,
Me and Paddy and mad Mick McPhew
All bound for Timbuckthree.

The captain was a scurvy knave
With a black patch on his nose,
He had a hook eye and a wooden-legged parrot
And rings on all of his toes.

The first mate was an ugly swab
His nose was lumpy and fat,
He was four foot four from his bald head to the floor
With a beard like an old doormat.

The old canal was wild that night
The waves they rocked the boat.
'Switch off the engine!' the captain cried,
So Paddy untied the goat.

The wind it tore off the captain's vest
And filled the toilet paper sails,
And Mad Mick sat in the old Crow's nest
A chewin' of his nails.

The Crow didn't like it so she gave him a shove
And he tumbled off, heading for the deck,
And if the captain hadn't broken his fall
Poor Mick would have broken his neck

We did four knots by the old gas works,
We sailed past the coal man's yard,
Then we ran ashore on a rusty old pram
That wasn't marked on the chart.

'All feet on deck!' the captain cried.
'Sorry I mean all hands!
We're sinking quick – a band on ship!'
But we couldn't see any band!

'Every man for himself!' the captain cried
The first mate his prayers did roar.
But me and the lads got some bars of soap
And washed ourselves ashore.

So that was the end of the Captain Bold
And the end of the *Bumblebee*,
And we waited at the old bus stop
For the half-past four bus to Timbuckthree.

Mike Harding

Short Visit, Long Stay

The school trip was a special occasion
But we never reached our destination
Instead of the zoo
I was locked in the loo
On an M62 Service Station.

Paul Cookson

The Great Escape

In the Great Escape from London Zoo
eight caribou and gnu they knew
mounted a minor military coup,
an act of animal derring-do,
and locked the staff they overthrew
in the 'potamus pit and a portaloo,
then caught a plane to North Peru.

As animals broke out two-by-two
to squeal and growl and grunt and moo
a loud unruly queue soon grew
that wriggled and ran and crawled and flew,
stampeding down the avenue.

In the Great Escape from London Zoo
we heard how a herd of kangaroo
had bid the big brown owl adieu
with a: 'Toodle-oo, mate, toodle-oo!'
but before he'd time to twit-tu-woo
they'd hopped it, heading for Timbuktu
and the owl himself had flown off too.

While a crocodile and a cockatoo
crossed the Thames in a slim canoe,
rowed by the bird, so the croc could chew . . .
chew through the bones of the eight-man crew
till the river ran red instead of blue.

In the Great Escape from London Zoo
the pandas abandoned their bamboo
and, all dressed up as railway crew,
hijacked the fifteen fifty-two
from platform three at Waterloo
and 'parley-voo' they zoomed straight through
Paris, and on to Katmandu.

Panic ensued and ballyhoo
when pot-bellied pig and rare-breed ewe
gatecrashed a very posh barbecue
terribly upsetting the well-to-do
and causing a heck of a hullabaloo.

You doubt my word? What's wrong with you?
Why, every detail here is true.
The Great Escape from London Zoo.
When was that? I thought you knew:
Years ago, at half-past two.

Nick Toczek

Tasting the Sea

Apparently
there were Cornish sea captains
who could tell exactly where they were
when mist and lack of lights conspired
to hide the coast from view.
When a storm had locked them
on a course for rocks,
they could tell which shore
they were heading towards
by tasting the sea.

And these old soaks,
these old sea rovers
would command the first mate
to hang overboard
and scoop up a cup of sea.
Then holding it up to the light
they'd argue over the colour.
They'd sniff, take a sip,
then swirl it about in the mouth
before spitting it out,
till one of their number
with further thought would announce:

Too bitter for Lizard,
too salty for Sennen,
too clean for Pendeen
too clear for Porthmear

It's here we are, he'd say
with certainty, jabbing a finger
down on the chart.
Then heads would nod
and an order be given
to turn the ship for home,
with a ration of rum for everyone
to celebrate
their escape.

Brian Moses

Postcard from Lilliput

Much news but
little space
on Lilliput
cards, so use
imagination.
Gulliver.

Debjani Chatterjee

K

Kissing and Other Things Best Avoided

Hugger Mugger

I'd sooner be
Jumped and thumped and dumped

I'd sooner be
Slugged and mugged . . . than *hugged* . . .

And clobbered with a slobbering
Kiss by Auntie Jean:

You know what I mean:

Whenever she comes to stay,
You know you're bound

To get one.
A quick
  short
  peck
  would
  be
  OK
But this is a
Whacking great
Smacking great
Wet one!

All whoosh and spit
And crunch and squeeze
And '*Dear* little boy!'
And 'Auntie's missed you!'
And 'come to Auntie, she
Hasn't *kissed* you!'
Please don't do it, Auntie,
PLEASE!

Or if you've absolutely
Got to,

And nothing on *earth* can persuade you
Not to,

The trick
Is to make it
Quick,

You know what I mean?

For as things are
I really would far,

Far sooner be
Jumped and thumped and dumped,

I'd sooner be
Slugged and mugged . . . than *hugged* . . .

And clobbered with a slobbering
Kiss by my Auntie

Jean!

Kit Wright

Victoria's Poem

Send me upstairs without any tea,
refuse me a plaster to stick on my knee.

Make me kiss Grandpa who smells of his pipe,
make me eat beetroot, make me eat tripe.

Throw all my best dolls into the river.
Make me eat bacon and onions – with liver.

Tell Mr Allan I've been a bad girl,
rename me Nellie, rename me Pearl.

But don't, even if
the world suddenly ends,
            ever again,
                    Mother,
wipe my face with a tissue
in front of my friends.

Fred Sedgwick

Lovey-dovey

When Dad and Mum go all lovey-dovey
we just don't know where to look.
My sister says, 'Cut it out you two,'
while I stick my nose in a book.

Mum has this faraway look on her face
while Dad has a silly grin.
'You don't have to mind us, kids,' he says.
We just wish they'd pack it in.

Dad calls Mum, 'Little Sugarplum';
and Mum says, 'You handsome brute.'
Dad laughs and says, 'Look at your Mum,
'don't you think that she's cute?

'I guess that's why I married her,
she's my truly wonderful one.'
Mum says he doesn't mean any of it
but she thinks he's a lot of fun.

I just can't stand all the kissing,
at their age they ought to know better.
I think I'll go up to my room
and write *Jim'll Fix It* a letter.

I hate it when they're lovey-dovey
but I hate it more when they fight
when faces redden and tempers flare
and sharp words cut through the night.

I'd rather they kissed and cuddled
and joked about and laughed,
at least we can tell everything's OK
when Mum and Dad are daft.

Brian Moses

A Hot Time in the Supermarket

When my mum gave my dad
The juiciest, most romantic kiss
Right there in the supermarket

And worse
Began to quickstep him down the aisle
To their favourite tune

I couldn't believe it.
Everybody stared.
My cheeks began to burn.

In our basket
The hot chilli sauce sweated
Ice cream melted
Ten frozen fish fingers defrosted
The fizzy wine popped its cork
The tomato sauce went redder
The tinned salmon pinker
The cream of mushroom soup
Boiled over
And the chicken drumsticks
Beat out a tango.

I had to have
Three tins of pop from the cold shelf
Two ice lollies
And a big swig of natural spring water
Just to get over it.

                              David Harmer

207

Parents!

Parents!
They're so embarrassing.

When my dad sneezes,
He makes such a racket
It's as if a minor explosion
Has been detonated
Inside his nose.
Then he whips out
His handkerchief with a flourish
And trumpets loudly,
Shattering the silence
With his coughing, spluttering and wheezing.

As for my mum,
Her stomach gurgles and rumbles
Like a broken cistern
That never stops filling.
It saves the loudest churnings
For that moment's silence
In the middle of a concert
Or the most dramatic moment
At the climax of a play,
So people turn and frown
Or pretend not to notice,
Though they couldn't help but have heard.
And I go bright red,
Wishing the ground would open up

And swallow me,
Or that I was cool and confident enough
To look disdainful,
As if to say:
She's not my mum, you know,
Don't blame me!

Parents!
They're so embarrassing.

John Foster

Licking Toads

'What I want to know is this,'
said Sharon. 'Is kissing Barry Reynolds
worse than licking toads,
or do they rate about the same
on any top ten list of hates?'
So we did a survey, round
all the girls in our year.
'Would you rather the toad or Barry?'
And everyone had to answer
or Sharon threatened to twist
their arms, but Melissa said
it was cruel to go on about Barry,
and we poked fun and said,
'You going to marry him are you?'
And then, when we counted
the votes, it seemed most girls
preferred to chance the toad
than risk kissing Barry.
Sharon said, 'You'd catch less
from the toad.' And then we said,
'Let's try again, would you rather
eat a tarantula egg omelette?'
But no one was quite
so sure about that!

Brian Moses

What Teachers Wear in Bed!

It's anybody's guess
what teachers wear in bed at night,
so we held a competition
to see if any of us were right.

We did a spot of research,
although some of them wouldn't say,
but it's probably something funny
as they look pretty strange by day.

Our headteacher's quite old fashioned,
he wears a Victorian nightshirt,
our sports teacher wears her tracksuit
and sometimes her netball skirt.

That new teacher in the infants
wears bedsocks with see-through pyjamas,
our deputy head wears a T-shirt
he brought back from the Bahamas.

We asked our secretary what she wore
but she shooed us out of her room,
and our teacher said, her favourite nightie
and a splash of expensive perfume.

And Mademoiselle, who teaches French,
is really very rude,
she whispered, 'Alors! Don't tell a soul,
but I sleep in the ... back bedroom!

Brian Moses

Blow This

Who
knows
why a
nose has
hair? Don't
despair for
it's   there
to   deter
the entry of
dust   which
turns to a crust,
clogs   nostrils
and blocks off
t h e a i r

Gina Douthwaite

My Mums Wears a Jelly Bra

My mum wears a jelly bra.
She says it helps her figure.
I reckon, she has matching pants
That make her bottom quiver.

Karen Costello-McFeat

A Sumo Wrestler Chappy

A sumo wrestler chappy
One day in the ring was unhappy
When thrown to the ground
His mum pinned him down
And in view of the crowd changed his nappy.

Paul Cookson

L

Love, Death, War and Peace

Great Sun

Great sun
Eat the clouds up
So that my love can flourish with my garden,
So that my love, my love
And all the busy joy of greenery
Can flourish.

Storm wind
That brings the clouds
Huge and heavy, stifling up the heavens,
Push on, push them over
So that the flattened garden can be righted
And love recover.

Jenny Joseph

Your Smile

When you smiled last night
the sun came up.
In less time than it takes
to strike a match or touch a flame
the entire firmament was aglow.
I watched with amazement and delight.
It's not often you see a sunrise at
that time of day.

Alan Durant

Glove on a Spiked Railing

Rescued, out in the cold,
five knitted fingers'
frosty glitter
won't abandon hope
wherever now may be
the hand that fits them
wearing unfamiliar numbness
like a second skin.

They seem to say
exactly what I feel
without you,
stuck here, waving
to my other half,
not given up just yet
but frozen stiff.

John Mole

218

Thinking of You

Sometimes I think of you
the way that the thinnest
wisp of a cloud
teased out
to gauzy mist
drifts off across the blue,
but sometimes too
the dark sky loaded with thunder
presses down
like a slab of stone
which I lie under
thinking of you.

John Mole

The Prince and the Snail

Once, in a castle
a Prince loved a snail.
He painted the shell gold
and kept the snail in his pocket.

The King and the Queen
thought the Prince mad.
'It must be a difficult relationship,'
said the King.
'Why?' asked the Prince.
(Love makes you that way.)

The Queen said,
'Son, let's talk.
You see, there're certain things
you can do
and certain things
you cannot do
and, I'm afraid,
kissing a snail in public
is most definitely out.'

The Prince said to the snail,
'This is hopeless.
We'll have to run away.'
'Mmm,' said the snail.
(Again, love makes you that way.)

So the Prince ran away
with the golden snail.
They ran to the edge
of the land
and sat on the beach.

'Phew,' said the Prince.
'I'm out of breath.'
'Take me out of your pocket!'
gasped the snail.
'I'm suffocating!'

Then, in the sea,
a huge black monster appeared.
It looked at the Prince
and winked.
'A whale!' said the snail.
'What a flirt!' said the Prince.

That night the Prince
swam out to the whale.
The whale was as big as a castle.
'I love you!' said the Prince.
'Glug, glug!' said the snail.

'Why not live in my belly?'
gurgled the whale.
(You know how whales are.)
So the Prince crawled inside.
'It's dark,' said the Prince.
'I love you,' said the whale.

Once, in a belly,
a Prince loved a whale.
As if the belly were a pocket
and the Prince a golden snail.

Philip Ridley

Reincarnation

I'm
putting my name down
to come back
a cat
like our Cleo,

snooze
the whole of my next life away,
letting my pride and joy,
my tail,
find the warmest places,

that corner of the garden
where the sun lingers
round the roots of the laburnum,

that spot on the landing
where hot water pipes run
under the carpet;

whenever I want to
I'll stretch myself,
arching my back ecstatically,

dig my fine claws into
the bedside rug,
a plump cushion, someone's lap;

I'll go mooching and mousing
by the light of the moon

and come in any old time I like!

You can guarantee
someone will always
be there

to feed me, stroke me,
make me purr.

Matt Simpson

Ice Cream

I dreamt of having a dog.
A racing dog.
A chasing dog.
An obedient amazing dog.

I got Scruff.
A rough dog.
A tough dog.
A run-in-circles-and-woof dog.

We were mates.

We liked the same things.
We liked running around the park.
We liked lying around the house.
And we liked eating,
especially ice cream.

We'd tried crisps
but they made him cough.
Shared sherbet made him foam.
Toffee stuck his teeth together.
Chocolate was one gulp and gone.
But ice cream . . .

He'd come running and smack his lips
then he'd be all laps and licks
and wags and shudders and shivers.
He became one huge wag of pleasure.
One excited quiver.

Sounds of bells on Saturday announce the ice cream van.
Across the busy street I go, coins hot in my hand.
'Ice cream cornet please – with raspberry sauce.'
Then Scruff comes running and smack. Of course. A car
Hits him full speed on.

One startled yelp, one shudder and he's gone.
Not the slightest movement now. Not the smallest sound.
Ice cream melting on to my foot.
Raspberry sauce sticky as blood.

Michaela Morgan

Canary

The dome of his head
Is round as an egg.
His skull as delicate as shell,
The bones inside his little body
Fine as pins.

I can spread his yellow wings
Like feather fans,
But he won't sing.
Not again. Not ever.
He is light as dust
And I must bury him.

His bright body
Like sunshine in a box
Deep in the shade
Of dark rhododendrons.
Muffled. Silent.
In the soft black soil.

Jan Dean

It's Spring Again

It's spring again,
But this year everything's different.
Grandad's vegetable patch isn't dug
And the man who came to mow the lawn
Didn't do it in stripes
Like Grandad did.

When I went with Grandma
To visit Grandad's grave,
The daffodils we planted in the autumn
Were in full bloom.
'He'd have liked them,
Wouldn't he, Grandma?' I said.
'Yes,' she said. 'He would have.'

John Foster

That Mouth

That mouth
was generous with kisses.

That mouth
was rich with tall tales.

That mouth
was at home with grapes.

That mouth
was a wealth of jokes.

Now that mouth
will say no more

will laugh no more.
And the silence hurts.

John Agard

Sensing Mother

Dad keeps Mum's favourite dress
deep in the bottom of the ottoman.
Sometimes, when he is at work
I stand listening to the tick of the clock
then go upstairs.

And propping up
the squeaky wooden lid, I dig through
layers of rough, winter blankets
feeling for that touch of silk.
The blue whisper of it cool
against my cheek.

Other times – the school-test times,
and Dad-gets-home-too-late-
to-say-goodnight times –
I wrap the arms of the dress around me,
breathing in a smell, faint as dried flowers.

I remember how she twirled around
– like a swirl of sky.

When I am old enough I will wear it.
Pulling up the white zip,
I'll laugh and spin,
calling out to my daughter:
How do I look?

Mandy Coe

Jack in the Sky

Jack popped his head through a door in the sky
Hopped down Memory Street
Raised his hat to the smiling sun
And the friends he chanced to meet.

He danced in the eye of the afternoon
Smiled at all he saw
While the cat on the sun-warmed doorstep purred
And licked her folded paw.

Jane on a swing in the garden green
Her yellow hair flowed free
Smiled at the ghost of brother Jack
That only she could see.

Gareth Owen

Sonnet Number One

The moon doth shine as bright as in the day
I sit upon the seesaw wondering why
She left me. Boys and girls come out to play.
But I'm bereft. I think I'm going to cry.
I gave her chocolate and I praised her skill
At skateboarding and football not to mention
Arm wrestling. As we slowly climbed the hill
To fetch some water, did I sense a tension?
She seemed preoccupied. She hardly spoke
And as we turned the handle to the well
I asked her, Jill, please tell me it's a joke.
She said, I've found another bloke. I fell,
I spun, head over heels into the dark
Down to the bottom where I broke my heart.

Roger Stevens

Paying His Respects

Great Grandad never talked
About the war.
'That,' he'd say with a sigh,
'That's over and done with.'

When I asked him
If the war was like the wars
In comics and in films,
He simply said,
'No, it was real.'

Every year
He got out his medals
And joined the parade
To the cenotaph,
Paying his respects.

John Foster

Just a Small War

We're watching the usual war pictures
On the six-o'clock news on the box:
Shells exploding, bodies lying,
Fires, tanks, roadblocks.
Dave says, 'Course, that's just a small war.
I'm not sure who's fighting who.
For real wars you have to go back
To World Wars One and Two.'

On the screen, in her shattered house,
A woman picks around for her stuff.

Bet she doesn't think it's a small war.
Bet she thinks it's real enough.

Eric Finney

From a Distance

I climbed to the top of the world today
and the world looked really small.
Guns and bombs and orphans' tears
couldn't be heard at all.
It all looked bright and beautiful
like a cheerful Christian hymn,
with enough green fields and shady woods
to put all the people in.

I couldn't see any fences
or signs which read 'Keep Out';
nor churned-up earth where tanks rolled through
to the enemy's victory shout.
And I couldn't see the eyes of a child
who had no tears left to cry,
or numb refugees at the side of the road
watch the flames from their homes light the sky.

I couldn't see the generals' smiles
as they met to divide up the land,
or hear the lies they told afterwards
with blood still warm on their hands.
I couldn't feel the sigh which leaks
from a million broken hearts
or the thick and sickening silence
before the next war starts.

I climbed to the top of the world today
and dreamed how the future could be:
the rivers unsullied by hatred and greed
and peace stretching clear to the sea.

Lindsay MacRae

Outbreak of Peace, Haiku

My mum declares peace.
She hands out bouquets of smiles.
Laughter like church bells.

Pie Corbett

Hope

Hope is the thing with feathers
That perches in the soul,
And sings the tune without the words,
And never stops at all,

And sweetest in the gale is heard;
And sore must be the storm
That could abash the little bird
That kept so many warm.

I've heard it in the chillest land,
And on the strangest sea;
Yet, never, in extremity,
It asked a crumb of me.

Emily Dickinson

M

Monsters, Ghosts and Ghouls

We Are Not Alone

When the floorboards creak and hinges squeak
When the TV's off but seems to speak
When the moon is full and you hear a shriek
We are not alone.

When the spiders gather beneath your bed
When they colonise the garden shed
When they spin their webs right above your head
We are not alone.

When the lights are out and there's no one home
When you're by yourself and you're on your own
When the radiators bubble and groan
We are not alone.

When the shadows lengthen round your wall
When you hear deep breathing in the hall
When you think there's no one there at all
We are not alone.

When the branches tap on your window pane
When the finger twigs scritch scratch again
When something's changed but it looks the same
We are not alone.

When the wallpaper is full of eyes
When the toys in the dark all change in size
When anything's a monster in disguise
We are not alone.

You'd better watch out whatever you do
There's something out there looking at you
When you think you are on your own
We are not
We are not
We are not alone.

Paul Cookson

Horribly Thin Poem

One winter evening,
When everything
Was dark,
And everyone was
Safely indoors,
I had to walk
Home
Alone,
All alone,
Through
Dark,
Cold,
Creepy,
Silent
Streets . . .

And I thought
Hello!
There's
A
Shadow . . .
A
Dark,
Mysterious shadow,
In that
Doorway
Over there . . .
What will I do

If the door
Opens
Just
As
I walk past,
And
A great
Ugly
HAND
Comes out
And grabs me?
What will I do?
WHAT will I do?
What WILL I do?
What will I DO?
And I ran
And ran
And ran
Right past that door.

And when I was past it,
I stopped
And looked back
And said:
'Ha ha!
You didn't get me that time!'

And a
Cold
Shivery
Croaky
Broken
Old voice
Slithered
Out of the letterbox
And said
'No, but just you wait,
There's always
Another
Time . . .'

David Orme

Quieter Than Snow

I went to school a day too soon
And couldn't understand
Why silence hung in the yard like sheets
Nothing to flap or spin, no creaks
Or shocks of voices, only air.

And the car park empty of teachers' cars
Only the first September leaves
Dropping like paper. No racks of bikes
No kicking legs, no fights,
No voices, laughter, anything.

Yet the door was open. My feet
Sucked down the corridor. My reflection
Walked with me past the hall.
My classroom smelt of nothing. And the silence
Rolled like thunder in my ears.

At every desk a still child stared at me
Teachers walked through walls and back again
Cupboard doors swung open, and out crept
More silent children, and still more.

They tiptoed round me
Touched me with ice-cold hands
And opened up their mouths with laughter
That was

Quieter than snow.

Berlie Doherty

Late Worker

Dad works on the night shift
he goes alone into the dark

He has no supper, Mum says
he gets a bite at work

but he tells us a story, tucks us in
and slips away like a shadow into shadows

He's always back by daybreak,
his long black coat hangs in the hall

but always his sad eyes, his great weariness
show how tiring the work must be

and why else would he need to sleep all day
in a wooden box in a cold cellar?

Dave Calder

It's Only the Storm

'What's that creature that rattles the roof?'
'Hush, it's only the storm.'

'What's blowing the tiles and branches off?'
'Hush, it's only the storm.'

'What's riding the sky like a wild white horse,
Flashing its teeth and stamping its hooves?'

'Hush, my dear, it's only the storm,
Racing the darkness till it catches the dawn.
Hush, my dear, it's only the storm.
When you wake in the morning, it will be gone.'

David Greygoose

Teasing Ghosts

They are behind me as I walk –
I can hear their whispery talk.
They make the twigs go crack,
and pull faces at my back.

I can feel them stare and stare –
but whenever I turn they're not . . .

Tim Pointon

Who's Afraid?

Do I have to go haunting tonight?
The children might give me a fright.
It's dark in that house.
I might meet a mouse.
Do I have to go haunting tonight?

I don't like the way they scream out
When they see me skulking about.
I'd rather stay here,
Where there's nothing to fear.
Do I have to go haunting tonight?

John Foster

Which Witch?

Two witches flew out on a moonlight night.
Their laughs were loud and their eyes were bright.
Their chins and their noses were pointed and long.
They shared the same broom and they sang the same song.
Their hats and their cloaks were as black as pitch,
And nobody knew which witch was which.

Julia Donaldson

The Ghoul School Bus

The ghoul school bus
is picking up its cargo
of little horrors.

They must all be home
before first light, when today
turns into tomorrow.

All the sons and daughters of vampires,
little Igors and junior Fangs,
the teenage ghouls with their ghoulfriends
all wail, as the bus bell clangs.

And the driver doesn't look well,
he's robed completely in black,
and the signboard says – 'Transylvania,
by way of hell and back'.

The seats are slimy and wet,
there's a terrible graveyard smell,
all the small ghouls cackle and spit,
and practise their ghoulish spells.

The witches are reading their ABCs,
cackling over 'D' for disease,
while tomboy zombies are falling apart
and werewolves are checking for fleas.

When the bus slows down to drop them off
at Coffin Corner or Cemetery Gates,
their mummies are waiting to greet them
with eyes full of anguish and hate.

The ghoul school bus
is picking up its cargo
of little horrors.

They must all be home
before first light, when today
turns into tomorrow.

Brian Moses

Little

It was a little thing,
such a little thing
and it begged me not to tell.
So I took it by the hand
and it led me into hell.

With almond eyes
– such startled eyes! –
it said it wouldn't hurt.
So I sandalled down the desperate stairs,
slipping on ancient dirt.

With coos and yelps
and triumphant smile
it posted me like a letter.
And here I am as sick as the dead
with no hope of getting better.

It was a little thing,
such a little thing
and it begged me not to tell.
So I took it by the hand
And it led me into hell.

Sue Stewart

It's Behind You

I don't want to scare you
But just behind you
Is a . . .

No! Don't look!
Just act calmly
As if it wasn't there.

Like I said
Can you hear me if I whisper?
Just behind you
Is a . . .

NO! DON'T LOOK!
Just keep on reading
Don't turn round, believe me
It isn't worth it.

If you could see
What I can see standing there
You'd understand.

It's probably one
Of the harmless sort
Although with that mouth
Not to mention the teeth
And all that blood
Dripping down its chin
I wouldn't like to say.

Oh listen
It's trying to speak
I think it wants to be friends.

Oh I see it doesn't, never mind
You'd better leave just in case
I expect you'll escape
If you don't look round.

Oh what a shame!
I thought you'd make it
To the door. Hard luck.
I still think it means no harm
I expect it bites all its friends.

David Harmer

The Teflon Terror

I know that the monster without a head
Is lying in wait right under my bed,
But being headless, he can't see
What I've brought upstairs with me.
This frying pan should do the trick.

BANG!

(Thank God that monster was non-stick!)

Andrew Fusek Peters

My Sister's a Monster

My sister's a monster –
It's true.
I know, because I've seen her change
From sugar and spice and oh-so-nice to

A raving, ranting beast
With bulging eyes
And long, wild hair;
I've even seen two horns appear
Out of her head, I swear.

Of course,
No one believes me when I tell them.
They think I'm just exaggerating,
Fabricating;
But that's because they never see
My sister's transformation
From human being into this thing.
Oh no. She keeps that certain revelation
Just for me.

You wait. One day soon
My sister will forget herself
In front of all our friends and family:
Her eyes will bulge
And two sharp horns will grow –
Then everyone will know
That my sister's a monster.

Gillian Floyd

I'm the Best Monster Around

My teacher yells and screams at me
Did you put glue in Sally's hair?
I smile and say
Why yes of course, do you see any other monsters here?

My mum looks crazed as she says
Did you spill the cream on dining room chair?
I grin evilly and say,
Why yes of course, do you see any other monsters here?

My nanny stomps her foot at me
Did you rip apart your sister's teddy bear?
I wrinkle my nose and say
Of course, do you see any other monsters here?

Being a monster is hard enough
When you live in this tiny town
But hey at least I can say
I'm the best Monster around!

Katherine Brandt

Horace the Horrid

The day that baby Horace hatched
his proud mum gave a ROAR,
then stomped around to show him off
to her monster friends next door.
She named him HORACE THE HORRID –
she was sure he'd be quite a lad –
but soon it was clear, to her horror,
that Horace just wasn't bad.

*You're supposed to EAT children, Horace,
not ask them out to play!
You're HORACE THE HORRID, Horace,
PLEASE put that teddy away!*

*Those feet are for kicking, Horace;
don't hide your claws under the mat!
That playpen's your BREAKFAST, Horace,
You're a MONSTER, remember that!*

I'm sorry, said Horace, bowing his head.
*I'm sorry to be such a bore,
but I'd rather eat carrots than children
and I really don't know how to roar.*
And he carried on humming his quiet hum
till his mother grew quite wild,
but Horace the Horrid just opened his mouth
and smiled and smiled and smiled.

He opened his gummy, grinny mouth
and smiled
   and smiled
      and smiled.

Judith Nicholls

Be Very Afraid

Of the Spotted Pyjama Spider
which disguises itself as a spot
on the sleeve of your nightwear,
waits till you fall asleep,
then commences its ominous creep
towards your face.

   Be very afraid
of the Hanging Lightcord Snake
which waits in the dark
for your hand to reach for the switch,
then wraps itself round your wrist
with a venomous hiss. Be afraid,

very afraid, of the Toothpaste Worm
which is camouflaged as a stripe of red
in the paste you squeeze
and oozes on to your brush
with a wormy guile
to squirm on your smile.

Be very afraid indeed
of the Bookworm Bat
which wraps itself like a dust jacket
over a book,
then flaps and squeaks on your face
when you take a look. Be afraid

of the Hairbrush Rat, of the Merit Badge Beetle,
of the Bubble Bath Jellyfish
and the Wrist Watch Tick (with its terrible nip)
of the Sock Wasp, of the Bee in the Bonnet
(camouflaged as the amber jewel
in the hatpin on it). Be afraid

of the Toilet Roll Scorpion,
Snug as a bug in its cardboard tube
until someone disturbs it,
of the Killer Earring Ant,
dangling from a lobe
until someone perturbs it. Don't be brave –

be very afraid.

Carol Ann Duffy

N

Nonsense

Hogging Hedgehogs

With thanks to Lewis Carroll

'Won't you trot a little faster?' said the hedgehog to the cat,
'The slugs are sliming frothily, there are earwigs brown and
    fat,
The snails are ripe for picking, there's a thousand grubs at
    least,
They are lurking in the compost heap, won't you come and
    join the feast?

'Will you, won't you, will you, won't you, will you join the
    feast?
Will you, won't you, will you, won't you, won't you join the
    feast?

'You really can't imagine how delightful it will taste
When we bite into a beetle, or a worm, so let's make haste!
When he thinks of hogging maggots a hedgehog almost runs,
For those that get there early get the fat and juicy ones!

'Will you, won't you, will you, won't you, will you join the
    feast?
Will you, won't you, will you, won't you, won't you join the
    feast?'

'I'm sure it sounds delicious,' his furry friend replied,
'So please enjoy your centipedes, with woodlice on the side,
But I've no need to join you, for I have a well-trained man,
And when I'm feeling hungry, why, he'll open up a can!

'I *will not, could not, will not, could not, will not join the
feast!*
I *will not, could not, will not, could not, could not join the
feast!*'

David Orme

The Pobble Who Has No Toes

I

The Pobble who has no toes
  Had once as many as we;
When they said, 'Some day you may lose them all;' –
  He replied, – 'Fish fiddle de-dee!'
And his Aunt Jobiska made him drink
Lavender water tinged with pink,
For she said, 'The World in general knows
There's nothing so good for a Pobble's toes!'

II

The Pobble who has no toes
    Swam across the Bristol Channel;
But before he set out he wrapped his nose
    In a piece of scarlet flannel.
For his Aunt Jobiska said, 'No harm
Can come to his toes if his nose is warm;
And it's perfectly known that a Pobble's toes
Are safe, – provided he minds his nose.'

III

The Pobble swam fast and well
    And when boats or ships came near him
He tinkledy-binkledly-winkled a bell
    So that all the world could hear him.
And all the Sailors and Admirals cried,
When they saw him nearing the further side, –
'He has gone to fish, for his Aunt Jobiska's
Runcible Cat with crimson whiskers!'

IV

But before he touched the shore,
    The shore of the Bristol Channel,
A sea-green Porpoise carried away
    His wrapper of scarlet flannel.
And when he came to observe his feet
Formerly garnished with toes so neat
His face at once became forlorn
On perceiving that all his toes were gone!

V

And nobody ever knew
   From that dark day to the present,
Whoso had taken the Pobble's toes,
   In a manner so far from pleasant.
Whether the shrimps or crawfish gray,
Or crafty Mermaids stole them away –
Nobody knew; and nobody knows
How the Pobble was robbed of his twice five toes!

VI

The Pobble who has no toes
   Was placed in a friendly Bark,
And they rowed him back, and carried him up,
   To his Aunt Jobiska's Park.
And she made him a feast at his earnest wish
Of eggs and buttercups fried with fish; –
And she said, – 'It's a fact the whole world knows,
That Pobbles are happier without their toes.'

Edward Lear

A Plea from an Angel

'I want to be *different*!
I want to wear brown –
And strum on a banjo –
And fly upside down . . .'

Trevor Harvey

Lettuce Marry

Lettuce Marry

Do you carrot all for me?
My heart beets for you,
With your turnip nose
And your radish face.
You are a peach.
If we cantaloupe
Lettuce marry;
Weed make a swell pear.

Anon.

The Cow

The cow stood on the hillside,
Its skin as smooth as silk,
It slipped upon a cowslip
And sprained a pint of milk.

Anon.

Adam and Eve and Pinch-Me

Adam and Eve and pinch-me
Went down to the river to bathe.
Adam and Eve were drowned –
Who do you think was saved?

Anon.

Ladles and Jellyspoons

Ladles and Jellyspoons

Ladles and Jellyspoons,
I come before you
To stand behind you
And tell you something
I know nothing about.
Next Thursday
Which is Good Friday
There'll be a Mothers' Meeting
For Fathers only.
Wear your best clothes if you haven't any
And if you come
Please stay at home.
Admission free
Pay at the door
Take a seat
And sit on the floor.
It makes no difference where you sit
The man in the gallery is sure to spit.

Anon.

Crazy Days

'Twas midnight on the ocean,
Not a streetcar was in sight;
The sun was shining brightly,
For it rained all day that night.

'Twas a summer day in winter
And snow was raining fast,
As a barefoot boy with shoes on
Stood sitting in the grass.

Anon.

One Fine Day in the Middle of the Night

One fine day in the middle of the night
Two dead men got up to fight.
Back to back they faced each other,
Drew their swords and shot each other.

Anon.

As I Was Going Out One Day

As I was going out one day
My head fell off and rolled away.
But when I saw that it was gone,
I picked it up and put it on.

And when I got into the street
A fellow cried: 'Look at your feet!'
I looked at them and sadly said:
'I've left them both asleep in bed!'

Anon.

A Tree Toad Loved a She-toad

A tree toad loved a she-toad
  That lived up in a tree.
She was a three-toed tree toad
  But a two-toed toad was he.
The two-toed toed tried to win
  The she-toad's friendly nod,
For the two-toed toad loved the ground
  On which the three-toed toad trod.
But no matter how the two-toed tree toad tried,
  He could not please her whim.
In her tree-toad bower,
  With her three-toed power
The she-toed vetoed him.

Anon.

Who's That Knocking on My Ring, Says the Chin

Who's that knocking on my ring, says the chin.
Me, says the stranger, I want to come in.

Selina Hill

River Don

How fortunate is Don
to have a river named after him.
I wish I had something
named after me.
River Brian doesn't sound quite right,
nor does Brian Street or Brian Road.
(There was a Brian Close once
but he was a cricketer.)
Scotland do interesting things with names.
I'd love to be the Pass of Brian
Or the Bridge of Brian – that sounds good.
The name Brian means strength,
tough as cowhide, strong as iron.
Maybe I could be the Mountain of Brian.
If I wanted it to reflect the very core of me,
the very heart, if I wanted it to conjure up
the very Brianness of Brian,
I'd find the River Brian flowing in my veins,
Fortress Brian in the heart of me,
Church of Brian in my soul.
And in my eyes, The Great Fire of Brian,
to be glimpsed by everyone
and admired!

Brian Moses

O

Ourselves and Others

The Cheer-up Song

No one likes a boaster
And I'm not one to boast,
But everyone who knows me knows
That I'm the most.

I'm the most attractive, I'm
The Media Superstar,
One hundred per cent in-tell-i-gent
And pop-u-lar.

All my jokes are funny.
Every one's a laugh.
Madonna pays me money for
My au-to-graph.

For I'm the snake's pyjamas, I'm
The bumble-bee's patella,
I'm a juicesome peach at a picnic on the beach, I'm
The rainmaker's umbrella.

Yes I'm the death-by-chocolate, I'm
The curried beans on toast,
And everyone who knows me knows that
I'm the most.

Tee-rr-eye-double-eff-eye-see
Triffic! TRIFFIC! TRIFFIC!
Yes it's me! ME! MEEE!

John Whitworth

First and Foremost

My good points:
I am fresh, novel,
the genuine article.
I am unprecedented.
From the word go
– a healthy ego;
I'm incomparable,
bold and original.
Never backwards
in coming forwards.
Never put
off to tomorrow
what I can do
today. I rise at dawn
with the cockerel.
I reap the first fruits.
I put my good foot first.
I also first-foot.
I am phenomenal.
First among equals.

I took the first step.
I made the first move.
I always stand up
to be counted.
I don't run away
from the truth.
I get things first
hand; I come straight
to the point.
Hold on, hold on,
I say, *first things first*.
To sum up:
I'm quite exceptional.

My bad points:
I am first
to fly off the handle.
I am selfish, callous,
cruel, ruthless.
I look after number one.
I put myself first.
My friends call me
Numero Uno.
It pains me, but doesn't stop
me pushing
to be first in the queue. *Oh!*
I say snootily,
first come first served.
I don't care for
other numbers.

Useless losers.
I travel first class.
I throw the first stone.
I am tall, lanky,
wear my beret
the French way.
I am Premier.
I am the first in my field.
I show off at first nights.
I believe in yours truly;
the first stroke
is half the battle.
Let's face things
frankly – I am the one
and only.

Jackie Kay

Isn't My Name Magical?

Nobody can see my name on me.
My name is inside
and all over me, unseen
like other people also keep it.
Isn't my name magical?

My name is mine only.
It tells I am individual,
the one special person it shakes
when I'm wanted.

Even if someone else answers
for me, my message hangs in air
haunting others, till it stops
with me, the right name.
Isn't your name and my name magic?

If I'm with hundreds of people
and my name gets called,
my sound switches me on to answer
like it was my human electricity.

James Berry

If Only I Were

The chameleon wind blowing over
   the rugged ranges of the Himalayas.

A tree in full regalia of autumn
   on a peacock-blue lake in Vermont.

A bee upon a raft of sunlight
   in the gardens of this nurturing earth.

A coral formation along the Great Barrier Reef.
   The robe of the night sky filigreed with stars.

A jugalbandi raga at dawn
   of sitar and shehnai, sarangi and tabla.

A wild flower greeting the weary
   explorer in some forgotten desert.

A rainbow poised over the Iguacu Falls
   Chanting *make me always the same as I am now.*

If only I were Mother Teresa's eyes
   watching over a sick, sleeping child.

A dream come true in the warm smiles
   of all the children in our world.

The healing hands of a surgeon,
    the defence of innocent folk.

The biting, trusting grip of a new-
    born child at the mother's breast.

The voices of poets, thinkers, artists, the words
    of inspiration in the struggle of our daily lives.

Shanta Acharya

Chameleon: tropical lizard that can change colour.
Great Barrier Reef: the largest coral reef in the world, in the Coral Sea off the coast of Australia.
Filigree: delicate ornamental work made from gold, silver or other fine twisted wire.
Jugalbandi raga: an Indian melody.
Sitar, shehnai, sarangi and tabla: Indian musical instruments.
Iguacu Falls: spectacular falls in southern Brazil, two and a half miles long and descending into the Iguacu River.
Mother Teresa: a saintly Catholic nun in Kolkata.

Colouring In

And staying inside the lines
Is fine, but . . .
I like it when stuff leaks –
When the blue bird and the blue sky
Are just one blur of blue blue flying,
And the feeling of the feathers in the air
And the wind along the blade of wing
Is a long gash of smudgy colour.
I like it when the flowers and the sunshine
Puddle red and yellow into orange,
The way the hot sun on my back
Lulls me – muddles me – sleepy
In the scented garden,
Makes me part of the picture . . .
Part of the place.

Jan Dean

The Boy Who Can't Get Out of Bed

is me.

The kid who draws
his curtains tight
on perfect afternoons
despite the heat

is me.

The lad whose pillow
keeps that hole
a head will leave
if left too long

is me.

The yob who speaks
in grunts, then dips
beneath the duvet
like a mole

is me.

The nipper's eyes
unused to light?
Whose pasty skin
could pass for milk?

Both mine.

The urchin told
his arms and legs
resemble strings?
That puny one

is me.

The boy whose parents
change entirely
downstairs, while he
is cast adrift

is me.

I will not move.
I will not change.
I will not leave
my bed; my bed

is me
is me
is me.

Stephen Knight

My Heart Has Been Broken

My heart has been broken,
My knuckles are rapped,
My head's in a whirl
My patience has SNAPPED!

My stomach's churned over,
My pride's hit the deck –
No wonder I'm *speechless*:

My body's a WRECK!

Trevor Harvey

What Will I Be When I Grow Up?

Mum said: 'Happy.'
Dad said: 'Older – and taller.'
My sister Kate said: 'Just as . . . nice!'
My mate Sam said: 'Still my best friend.'
My aunty Jessie said: 'Anything you want to be.'
My uncle Jack said: 'An adult!'
My teacher said: 'Wiser.'
My Gran said: 'Brilliant.'
Doesn't anybody know?

James Carter

Amazing Inventions

When I was 10
I really believed
that by the time
I was 20
there would be
such amazing inventions as
flying cars
underwater cars
machines that could make any flavour crisp you asked for
day trips to the moon
video phones and
robot dogs and cats
in every home
and
most importantly
bubble gum
that could make you
invisible

So you can imagine
just how disappointed I was
when I got to 20
and none of them
had come true

So you can also imagine
how extremely disappointed I was
when I got to 40
and still none of them
had come true
either

Until they do
I'd like to say
Do you know what
I think
is the most amazing invention
us humans
have come up with so far?

Have a think

Our brains
come up with them

Our mouths
get rid of them

This poem
is made of them

James Carter

Inside

Now
you
may think
I'm walking tall
I'm talking big
I've got it all –
but here inside
I'm ever so shy
I sometimes cry
I'm curled in a ball
I'm no feet small
no   I'm
not   big
not   tall
at   all

James Carter

The Clouds Bunch Quietly

the clouds bunch quietly –
I wait alone
after missing the bus

Gary Hotham

Two Trains

Two carriages side by side
About to depart in the darkness:

There's me
Looking into the other,

Expecting to find
My own reflection,

Shocked
To find not my own

But a stranger
Looking into my eyes.

Rody Gorman

The Secret Brother

Jack lived in the green-house
When I was six,
With glass and with tomato plants,
Not with slates and bricks.

I didn't have a brother,
Jack became mine.
Nobody could see him,
He never gave a sign.

Just beyond the rockery,
By the apple-tree,
Jack and his mother lived,
Only for me.

With a tin telephone
Held beneath the sheet,
I would talk to Jack each night.
We would never meet.

Once my sister caught me,
Said, 'He isn't there.
Down among the flower-pots
Cramm the gardener

Is the only person.'
I said nothing, but
Let her go on talking.
Yet I moved Jack out.

He and his old mother
Did a midnight flit.
No one knew his number:
I had altered it.

Only I could see
The sagging washing-line
And my brother making
Our own secret sign.

Elizabeth Jennings

When Your Face Doesn't Fit

When your face doesn't fit
What can be done?
You can't go shopping
To buy a new one.

If you prefer work
And your class prefers play
If you dress in yellow
And they dress in grey

If your class are all bored
But you are excited
And you support City
But they cheer United

When you walk to school
Go in the school gate
And they come by car
And then lie in wait

To call out your name
And to laugh and to hit
What do you do
When your face doesn't fit?

Can you tighten a screw
And adjust it a bit?
Is that what you do
When your face doesn't fit?

Roger Stevens

Duncan Gets Expelled

There are three big boys from primary seven
who wait at the main school gate with stones
in their teeth and names in their pockets.
Every day the three big boys are waiting.
'There she is. Into her, boys. Hey, Sambo.'

I dread the bell ringing, and the walk home.
My best friend is scared of them and runs off.
Some days they shove a mud pie into my mouth.
'That's what you should eat,' and make me eat it.
Then they all look in my mouth, prodding a stick.

I'm always hoping we get detention.
I'd love to write 'I will be better' 400 times.
The things I do? I pull Agnes MacNamara's hair.
Or put a ruler under Rhona's bum and ping it back
till she screams; or I make myself sick in the toilet.

Until the day the headmaster pulls me out,
asking all about the three big boys.
I'm scared to open my mouth.
But he says, 'You can tell me, is it true?'
So out it comes, making me eat the mud pies.

Two of them got lines for the whole of May.
But he got expelled, that Duncan MacKay.

Jackie Kay

Tea

Chipped white china mug
The casualty of some Great War.
The making of the tea,
An act of Reconciliation
Designed to ally the forces.
The tea bag hovers on the surface,
A bruise against soft milky skin
Before fading to the bottom
So no-one would know it had ever been.
I make this tea for you
To devour in one long gulp.
As I take it to you, it scalds my fingers.

Olivia Goddard

P
People and Places

Kirk Deighton

Kirk Deighton?
That can't be the name of a place!
Sounds more like the name
of a superhero, a '00' agent,
someone to swoon over.
Kirk Deighton,
suave, sophisticated,
a gold-plated gun in a shoulder holster,
hairy chest, bulletproof vest.
The kind of guy that girls adore,
a secret spy on a dangerous mission
somewhere off the A1, south Yorkshire.

Brian Moses

A Proper Poet

Today we have a real-live poet in school –
This gentleman who's standing next to me.
I must say when I met him in the entrance,
He was not as I imagined he would be.

I'd always thought that poets were tall and wan,
With eyes as dark and deep as any sea,
So when I saw this jolly little man,
He didn't seem a proper poet to me.

294

The poets I've seen in pictures dress in black
With velvet britches buttoned at the knee,
So when I saw the T-shirt and the jeans,
He didn't look a proper poet to me.

I've read that famous poets are often ill,
And die consumptive deaths on a settee.
Well I'd never seen a healthier-looking man
He just didn't look a proper poet to me.

My favourite poems are by Tennyson and Keats.
This modern stuff is not my cup of tea,
So when I heard our poet was keen on rap
He didn't sound a proper poet to me.

Well, I'm certain that we'll all enjoy his poems
And listen – after all we've paid his fee –
I hope that they're in verses and they rhyme
For that is proper poetry – to me.

Gervase Phinn

Identifying Things

Davy loved natural history –
He wandered round for hours,
Identifying birds and bees,
Identifying flowers.

He knew the names of orchids –
He identified each one,
He identified each butterfly
That settled in the sun.

He knew the names of spiders,
Of beetles, worms and grubs,
He identified the leafy trees,
The grasses, ferns and shrubs.

He knew the names of songbirds,
He identified each tweet –
The wren, the thrush, the wall-creeper,
The ring-necked parakeet.

He knew the name of lizards,
Of snakes and snails too,
He roamed the world, identifying
Species old and new.

Then one day in the mountains
Davy saw something gleam.
He lifted his binoculars
Then gasped . . . was this a dream?

For looking down at Davy
From the canyon's rocky rim
Was a vulture with a telescope –
Identifying him!

Richard Edwards

Stirring Times

Families weren't small.
Isabella Beeton
could rustle up a meal
just starting with

the head of a hog

a pint of cream

two dozen eggs . . .

and still know
that nothing would be left
uneaten.

Judith Nicholls

Auntie Betty Thinks She's Batgirl

Auntie Betty pulls her cloak on
And the mask – the one with ears.
Almost ready, check the lipstick,
Wait until the neighbours cheer.
Through the window. What a leap!
She lands right in the driver's seat.
Off she goes with style and grace
To make our world a better place.

Andrea Shavick

For Years I Asked Uncle Harry

For years I asked Uncle Harry
Why he wouldn't, but he'd just say,
'Maybe I will some time soon,
I'm not in the mood today.'

But I pestered my Uncle Harry
Till eventually he did,
And suddenly there was chaos,
The cat ran away and hid

Inside the Rottweiler's kennel,
The fish all jumped out of the pond,
The parrot in its cage screamed, 'Let me out!'
And the blackbird in the garden went blond.

A squirrel in a tree near the window
Just keeled over and died,
And the doctor's been treating me for shock
Since my Uncle Harry smiled.

Valerie Bloom

My Uncle Percy Once Removed

My Uncle Percy once removed
his bobble hat, scarf, overcoat,
woolly jumper, string vest,
flared trousers and purple Y-fronts
and ran onto the pitch at Wembley
during a Cup Final
and was at once removed
by six stewards and nine officers of the law.
Once they'd caught him.

Paul Cookson

Mistress Cooper

A hat-fanatic, a hat-fanatic,
Mistress Cooper is a hat-fanatic,
every hat she sees she has to have it.
Who knows how she got the hat-habit.

High hats, low hats,
fat hats, skinny hats,
springy hats, frilly hats,
cocky hats, floppy hats.
Hats in hat-boxes, hats on hat-racks,
a hundred and twenty-two to be exact.

'How's that for a hat?' she'll say to you,
whenever she wears a hat that is new.
If you value the friendship of Mistress Cooper
simply answer, 'It's super-dooper.'

Grace Nichols

Mrs Dungeon Brae

Mrs Dungeon Brae lived on the Isle of Mull,
the fairest of the rarest,
of all the western isles,
in a ramshackle farm house,
close to the hoarse heaving sea.

Every morning Mrs Dungeon Brae
was up with her white goats
pulling their teats for thin milk.
If she stumbled across a stranger
on her acre of land,

she reached for her gun, an old
long gun that belonged to her father,
his father before him, his father before him.
Then fired in the fern-scented air;
and watched the crows and stranger scatter.

She laughed a grim dry cough of a laugh.
Her face had all of Scotland's misery –
every battle fought and lost;
but her cheeks were surprises – a dash
of colour, a sprig of purple heather

peeping over the barren hillside.
Once, alone, in her house,
she sat down in her armchair
with her grey hair yanked into a bun
and died –

A tight, round ball of a death.
And nobody found her:
everybody was terrified of trespassing.
So the skeleton of Mrs Dungeon Brae
sits on her favoured armchair,

And the radio is playing Bach.
Ach. Ach.
Mrs Dungeon Brae.
The strings haunting the bones of Mrs Dungeon
Brae.
Ach. Ach. Mrs Dungeon Brae. Ach. Ach.

Jackie Kay

Limerick

A woman named Mrs S. Claus
Deserves to be heard from because
She sits in her den
Baking gingerbread men
While her husband gets all the applause.

J. Patrick Lewis

The Blacksmith

Got tired of all the noise –
The hammer's clashing beat,
Got tired of all the smoke –
The spark-showers and the heat,
Got tired of all the beasts –
Their stamp-stamp and their stare,
Got tired of all the sweat
And the red coals' glare.

Went down to the sea one day,
Heard the water sing,
Took off all his clothes,
His apron, everything,
Waded out and dived
With seals and porpoises,
Set up shop on a reef to make
Shoes for sea horses.

Richard Edwards

The Giantess

Where can I find seven small girls to be pets,
where can I find them?
One to comb the long grass of my hair
with this golden rake,
one to dig with this copper spade
the dirt from under my nails.
I will pay them in crab-apples.

Where can I find seven small girls to help me,
where can I find them?
A third to scrub at my tombstone teeth
with this mop in its bronze bucket,
a fourth to scoop out the wax from my ears
with this platinum trowel.
I will pay them in yellow pears.

Where can I find seven small girls to be good dears,
where can I find them?
A fifth one to clip the nails of my toes
with these sharp silver shears,
a sixth to blow my enormous nose
with this satin sheet.
I will pay them in plums.

But the seventh girl will stand on the palm of my hand,
singing and dancing,
and I will love the tiny music of her voice,
her sweet little jigs.
I will pay her in grapes and kumquats and figs.
Where can I find her?
Where can I find seven small girls to be pets?

Carol Ann Duffy

Giant's Eye View

(From the Grossmunster Tower, Zurich)

It's great to get a giant's eye view
of this city,
people down below not knowing
they're watched . . .

It'd like to reach down
and rearrange the streets.
Like a mischievous giant with elastic arms
I could de-rail trams, cause traffic jams,
move parked cars to different spaces,
wipe the smile from people's faces
by flipping them into the river
with my finger flicks . . .

With my giant's eye I could spy into skylights,
I could snoop in hidden courtyards.
I could block chimneys with my thumbs,
re-route smoke through the rooms below.

And all the birds thinking they're safe,
that the skyways belong to them . . .
Be gone gulls, scram pigeons,
there'll be no skywalking on my rooftops.

For one trifling moment
I'd be the hidden king of this city,
leave my giant's mark and feel the power
of the writer who scratched at the tower top:
ich war hier . . .
I WAS HERE!

Brian Moses

The Fantasy Kid

The Fantasy Kid chewed language like gum,
and stuck it all over the woodwork
where it turned hard, and people picked
at it with broken fingernails.

The Fantasy Kid worked words like clay:
great blobs and unfired sculptures
that changed in time to vases, pots, and jugs,
after you'd learnt to live with them.

The Fantasy Kid might never have existed,
but he walked into the lights one day,
and smiled at a handwritten friend
across a room of solid colours.

The Fantasy Kid laughed at the headlines.
Cut them up to make meaning, cut them down
to tell the truth. Stuck them all over
envelopes that flew out of his hand.

The Fantasy Kid woke up one morning
to see the summer disappearing over the horizon.
The storm that followed swallowed him,
and he was gone like a biro suddenly empty.

The Fantasy Kid left town. He's gone.
The mailbox is empty, the alphabet dust.
A bookshelf full of unwritten books
stands waiting for his return.

The Fantasy Kid is coming to your town.
Lock up your cider, put away your pens.
He'll teach your daughters to laugh,
your sons to read. Steal your voice.

Rupert M. Loydell

House Party

The houses had a party
they invited all their friends –
the semis and the terraced
the middles and the ends.
They invited all the chalets,
high-rise blocks of flats,
caravans and castles,
homes for dogs and cats.

They invited all the bungalows,
houses from Peru,
'scrapers from Big Apple,
huts from Timbuktu.
The igloos came,
the teepees,
pagodas and a cave,
an ant hill
and a beehive,
a police house
and a nave.

It was a lovely party –
the church house did some chants,
the summer house brought sunshine,
and the greenhouse brought the plants.
The lighthouse winked a message
for peace within each house . . .
'Hallelujah' sang the angels
'Hallelujah' sighed the mouse.

Peter Dixon

Voices . . .

'Come in!'
My mother's voice boomed across the backs of houses,
calling me home as dusk fell that July evening.
But still we played, four friends adventuring
at the end of Matthew's long, overgrown garden
where a tumbledown shed, half lost in waves of weeds,
was our pirate ship sailing uncharted seas.
Dirt-streaked, and oblivious of the deepening purple dark,
we played on as first stars blinked like harbour lights.
  'Come in!
  It's late!
  Come in!'

  'Come in!'
The boatman's hoarse voice reverberated
across the lake's sparkling, sunlit-wrinkled water.
Yet my cousins continued to row towards the reed beds
where ducks, moorhens and coots paddled and pecked.
We laughed as heavy oars dipped and splashed,
and gazed when a flight of geese took off, wings clapping.
The rowing boat rocked in the wind and waves,
and still the boatman's hand-cupped shout from the jetty,
  'Come in!
  Times's up!!
  Come in!'

'*Come in!*'
The crabbed old woman smiled toothlessly
as she invited the children lost in the green wood
to rest in her cottage half hidden in bushes and trees.
I remember how the storyteller added scary sound effects
– an owl's wavering hoot, wind hushing in the treetops,
and his fingers snapping like dead, woodland twigs.
Dry-mouthed and wide-eyed we stared intently
as he mimicked the witch's final invitation,
  '*Come in!*
  dear children.
  Come in!'

Wes Magee

The Big Shed

A ramshackle den of clutter,
A mazy mixture of the useful and the useless,
The rubbish, the rusty, the wood and the mud.

At least three small sheds' worth
Of tongue and groove and four by two,
Dismantled the flat packed . . . well, sort of . . .
All jumbled zig-zag seesaw heaps.

The monster orange rotavator,
Its giant teeth caked with mud
Silent and untamed
I was never allowed to grapple this beast
Until I was at secondary school.

The dead red and white motor scooter
Complete with windshield and crash helmet
That Dad could never get to work
But Cousin Paul took and resurrected.

Stacks and stacks and stacks
Of multi-purpose bamboo canes
That would become arrows, guns or swords
Depending on last night's television.

Hay bales, musty, dusty and precarious
Transformed into forts, mountains or sheer rock faces
Depending on last night's television.

The bowed wooden barrel we broke
One summer holiday afternoon
When trying to walk inside it, the barrel over our heads
Because we were re-enacting an adventure from 'Scooby
    Doo'.

The legend of 'Hairy Face'
Created then extended
From nothing to belief
Thanks to invented sightings and pretend happenings.
All scratchings, creakings and whistlings became his.
No one really believed
Until they were left alone at dusk
When darkness extended its bony fingers,
Squeezing out remaining light
And 'Hairy Face' lurked in every single shadow.

Hide-and-seek became a game
With endless possibilities.
No two games identical our options knew few limits
As plastic sheets, piles of planks,
Pallets and potato sacks
Chimney pots and high hay stacks
Were rearranged so that youthful bodies were concealed
    that little bit longer.

We could lose ourselves for hours
in this ramshackle den of clutter,
That mazy mixture of the rubbish and the rusty
The wood, the mud, the useful, the useless
And us.

Paul Cookson

South to North; 1965

I was born South of the river
down in the delta, beyond the bayou
lived in the swamps just off the High Street
London alligators snapping my ankles.

It was Bromley, Beckenham, Penge, Crystal Palace
where the kids said *wotcha*, ate bits of *cike*,
the land my father walked as a boy
the land his father walked before him.

I was rooted there, stuck in the clay
until we drove North, moved to Yorkshire
a land of cobbles, coal pits and coke works
forges and steel, fires in the sky.

Where you walked through fields around your village
didn't need three bus-rides to see a farm.

It was Mexbrough, Barnsley, Sprotbrough, Goldthorpe
I was deafened by words, my tongue struck dumb
gobsmacked by a language I couldn't speak in.

Ayop, sithee, it's semmers nowt
What's tha got in thi snap, chaze else paze?
Who does tha supoort, Owls else Blades?
Dun't thee tha me, thee tha thi sen
Tha's a rate un thee, giz a spice?

Cheese and peas, sweets and football
I rolled in a richness of newfound vowels
words that dazed, dazzled and danced
out loud in my head until it all made sense
in this different country, far away
from where I was born, South of the river.

David Harmer

Sunday Morning Diary Poem

This Sunday morning
surprised by birdsong.
Sun warms roofs,
casts cool sharp shadows –

though the road glitters.
Frost gilds
each
step.

Daisy and Teddy
run on ahead,
their voices echo
up the narrow lane
to Sunday school.

A marmalade cat
sneaks by greystone walls,
a blackbird sets off an alarm,
calls an early warning . . .

Trees are still skeletal,
form stark patterns
against a blue sky.

After weeks of grey fog
and sudden snow –
it feels good
to know the sun's
kindly glow –

to catch birdsong
as it drifts along
the lanes.

Pie Corbett

Home

East Anglia. Wind whipping in from the sea.
This is the place that is home to me.

  Dunes. Grass so coarse it hurts. Larks
hammering tall spring air over crumbling coastlines.
Views across fenland and heathland: cathedrals like liners
   where smiling angels hover
and other views across broadland in summer to barges
   sewing sky/land seams; and
   towns smelling of malt and hop.
Estuaries glinting like cheap jewellery.

No downs swinging deep into valleys and up to hilltops.
  No steep paths dropping to tiny harbours.

East Anglia. Wind whipping in from the sea.
This is the place that is home to me.

Fred Sedgwick

Map of India

If I stare at the country long enough
I can prise it off the paper,
lift it like a flap of skin.

Sometimes it's an Advent calendar –
each city has a window
which I leave open
a little wider each time.

India is manageable – smaller than
my hand, the Mahanadi River
thinner than my lifeline.

Moniza Alvi

Advent: a period including four Sundays before Christmas.
Mahanadi: an Indian river, its name means 'Great River'.

Q

Queens, Kings and Historical Stuff

Japheth's Notes: A Fragment

Blue wash
drifting to grey.
First waterdrops
on father's up-turned head,
dew on a web of thinning hair.
Mist gathers over Ararat.

Voices of man and animal
up-pitched by fear.
Hammers drum a crescendo.
Plaintive duo of wolves howl
their elegy for drowning world.
Waters rise over Ararat.

Nostrils sharp with
gopher wood and pitch,
damp fur and panic-sweat.
Paws and claws jostle,
trail mud and excrement.
Sweet-sour smell
of ripening oranges,
fermenting grape
and olive oil.
Lord, may we safely
sink to earth on Ararat.

Judith Nicholls

Roman Invaders

Where did all the Romans go?
After taking ancient Britain by storm
They came over here in short leather skirts
Then complained that they couldn't keep warm

They rubbed their bodies with stinging nettles
In an attempt to keep in the heat
But the endless drizzle and downpours of rain
Brought on their hasty retreat

They'd have known that it always rains
If they'd checked the weather report
But they jumped back into their long wooden boats
And sailed to a warmer resort.

Damian Harvey

A Liking for the Viking

I've always had a liking for the Viking;
His handsome horns; his rough and ready ways;
His rugged russet hair beneath his helmet
In those metal-rattle, battle-happy days.

I've always had a longing for a longboat;
To fly like a dragon through the sea
To peaceful evenings round a real fire,
Alive with legend; rich with poetry.

I've always had a yearning for the burning
Of brave flames irradiating valour;
For the fiery longboat carrying its Chieftain
To his final feast in glorious Valhalla.

Celia Warren

Castle to Be Built in the Woods

1. Choose a wood.

2. Make a clearing
   near a stream.

3. Dig a moat.
   Make it deep, wide.
   Fill it with water. One bridge only.

4. Lay solid foundations for your castle.
   Then build strong buttresses, stout keeps
   and tall towers with crenellations
   around the high battlements.

5. Make sure your castle has servants such as
   clerks, tailors, nurses, messengers,
   bootmakers, brewers, and a barber.
   You will need to lay down stores
   of food, wine, wax, spices and herbs.

6. An airy church inside the castle grounds
   and a dark dungeon deep below ground
   will mean that you can have
   Heaven and Hell at your fingertips.
   Don't forget to stock your arsenal with
   swords, daggers, lances, shields, battle-axes, etc.

7. Fire arrows at anyone who tries to
   attack your castle. Build murder-holes
   so that you can drop missiles and stones
   on the heads of your enemies.
   If you catch spies, lock them in
   the smallest, narrowest, smelliest room.
   Act ruthlessly. Behead people, frequently.

8. Hide treasure in a very secret part of the castle.
   Lock a beautiful princess in the tower.
   Force your fiercest dragon to guard both of these.
   Nominate a knight who will fight your battles
   so that you can never be injured or endangered.
   Employ a storyteller to make up tall tales
   and ghost stories about your castle.
   Marry someone and he can be the king.

John Rice

At Senlac Hill, 15 October 1066

Broken blades still bright with blood
fallen and flung far over the field,
the battered bodies of mangled men,
beaten by battle, bruised and bleeding
crying for care, or still as stones
their shields shattered, their spears scattered
their breathing butchered, spent and stopped,
lie heaped and piled in many mounds.

My sister and I search for our father
killed or captured, we don't know
but missing since midnight,
like Harold our King, now carrion crows
swoop and swirl over the fallen
pecking for pickings, our mother moans
weeps in her hands and holds her hair
away from her face, missing her man
amongst the many, the stiff and the still
or those who groan from their war-wounds.

Yesterday we were Saxons, English and angry
ready for riot against her foes
now we are Normans, French and fatherless
dazed and despairing, lost with dead
already our masters make preparations
digging their ditches to raise their ramparts
our future is dreaded, dismal and dull
stretched out in front of us like a dark day.

David Harmer

First Contact

The thick hair caressed her back
as she lifted her head,
And stared.

She reached her hand,
Annatto-stained, to the shoulder
Of her small dumb dog.

The parrots, for once,
Were silent,
Breaking off their bickering
To stare with her

Across the blue stillness,
To the three squares of white
Skirting the horizon.

She watched them race closer,
Big-bellied with the wind,
Saw the elaborate canoes beneath.

They were like nothing she had seen before,
So she dropped her digging stick,
And ran.

Valerie Bloom

The Powder Monkey

This is the moment I dread,
my eyes sting with smoke,
my ears sing with cannon fire.
I see the terror rise inside me,
coil a rope in my belly to keep it down.
I chant inside my head to free my nerve.

Main mast, mizzen mast, foremast,
belfry, capstan, waist.

We must keep the fire coming.
If I dodge the sparks
my cartridge will be safe,
if I learn my lessons
I can be a seaman,
if I close my eyes to eat my biscuit
I won't see the weevils.

Main mast, mizzen mast, foremast,
shock lockers, bowsprit, gripe.

Don't stop to put out that fire,
run to the hold,
we must fire at them
or they will fire at us.

Main mast, mizzen mast, foremast,
belfry, capstan, waist.

My mother never knew me,
but she would want to know this –
I can keep a cannon going,
I do not need her kiss.

Chrissie Gittins

Before 1794 children aged six and upwards went to sea. After 1794 the
minimum age was thirteen.

The Charge of the Light Brigade

I

Half a league, half a league,
   Half a league onward,
All in the valley of Death
   Rode the six hundred.
'Forward, the Light Brigade!
Charge for the guns!' he said;
Into the valley of Death
   Rode the six hundred.

II

'Forward, the Light Brigade!'
Was there a man dismay'd?
Not tho' the soldier knew
 Some one had blunder'd:
Theirs not to make reply,
Theirs not to reason why,
Theirs but to do and die:
Into the valley of Death
 Rode the six hundred.

III

Cannon to right of them,
Cannon to left of them,
Cannon in front of them
 Volley'd and thunder'd;
Storm'd at with shot and shell,
Boldly they rode and well,
 Into the jaws of Death,
 Into the mouth of Hell
 Rode the six hundred.

IV

Flash'd all their sabres bare,
Flash'd as they turn'd in air,
Sabring the gunners there,
Charging an army, while
   All the world wonder'd:
Plunged in the battery-smoke
Right thro' the line they broke;
   Cossack and Russian
Reel'd from the sabre-stroke
   Shatter'd and sunder'd.
Then they rode back, but not,
   Not the six hundred.

V

Cannon to right of them,
Cannon to left of them,
Cannon behind them
   Volley'd and thunder'd;
Storm'd at with shot and shell,
While horse and hero fell,
They that had fought so well
Came thro' the jaws of Death
Back from the mouth of Hell,
All that was left of them,
   Left of six hundred.

VI

When can their glory fade?
O the wild charge they made!
    All the world wonder'd.
Honour the charge they made!
Honour the Light Brigade,
    Noble six hundred!

Alfred, Lord Tennyson

America's Gate (Ellis Island)

'I'm bringing something beautiful to America,'
(Girl, 10 years)

If I miss my name
    then I might be forever knocking
        on America's gate.
If I lose my ticket and miss my turn
    I may never learn the lie of this land.
for all that I've planned
    is tied up in this trip,
all that I own
    is packed up in this bag.
And there isn't much money
    but there's gifts I can bring.
And I'm bringing them all to America,
I'm bringing them all from home.

Not my mother's rings
   or my party dress,
not my father's watch
   or my lacy shawl,
just the moon on my shoulder,
   a voice that can sing,
feet that can dance
   and a pipe that I play.
And I'm playing now for America,
   and I'm hoping that someone will notice.
Then perhaps I won't be here forever
knocking on America's gate.

Brian Moses

My Mother Saw a Dancing Bear

My mother saw a dancing bear
By the schoolyard, a day in June.
The keeper stood with chain and bar
And whistle-pipe, and played a tune.

And bruin lifted up its head
And lifted up its dusty feet,
And all the children laughed to see
It caper in the summer heat.

They watched as for the Queen it died.
They watched it march. They watched it halt.
They heard the keeper as he cried,
'Now, roly-poly!' 'Somersault!'

And then, my mother said, there came
The keeper with a begging-cup,
The bear with burning coat of fur,
Shaming the laughter to a stop.

They paid a penny for the dance,
But what they saw was not the show;
Only, in bruin's aching eyes,
Far-distant forests, and the snow.

Charles Causley

The Titanic

Under the ocean where water falls
over the decks and tilted walls
where the sea comes knocking at the great ship's door,
the band still plays
to the drum of the waves,
to the drum of the waves.

Down in the indigo depths of the sea
the white shark waltzes gracefully
down the water-stairway, across the ballroom floor
where the cold shoals flow,
and ghost dancers go,
ghost dancers go.

Their dresses are frayed, their shoes are lost,
their jewels and beads and bones are tossed
into the sand, all turned to stone,
as they sing in the sea
eternally,
eternally.

Currents comb their long loose hair,
dancers sway forever where
the bright fish nibble their glittering bones,
till they fall asleep
in the shivering deep,
in the shivering deep.

Gillian Clarke

Boy at the Somme

'The last one there is a cow pat!'
grinned the small boy
running between the white headstones
as he began the one hundred metre dash
along the narrow strip of turf separating
Private Tom Atkins, age 18, of the Lancashire Fusiliers,
from Lieutenant Edward Hollis, age 19,
of the Seaforth Highlanders;
more than twice the distance they managed
over the same small field
that October morning eighty-seven years before
into the spitting venom of the machine guns
that killed them instantly.

Alan Durant

The Gresford Disaster

You've heard of the Gresford disaster,
The terrible price that was paid,
Two hundred and forty-two colliers were lost
And three men of a rescue brigade.

It occurred in the month of September,
At three in the morning, that pit
Was racked by a violent explosion
In the Dennis where gas lay so thick.

The gas in the Dennis deep section
Was packed there like snow in a drift,
And many a man had to leave the coal-face
Before he had worked out his shift.

A fortnight before the explosion,
To the shot-firer Tomlinson cried
'If you fire that shot we'll be all blown to hell!'
And no one can say that he lied.

The fireman's reports they are missing,
The records of forty-two days;
The colliery manager had them destroyed
To cover his criminal ways.

Down there in the dark they are lying,
They died for nine shillings a day.
They have worked out their shift and now they must lie
In the darkness until Judgement Day.

The Lord Mayor of London's collecting
To help both our children and wives,
The owners have sent some white lilies
To pay for the poor colliers' lives.

Farewell, our dear wives and our children,
Farewell, our old comrades as well.
Don't send your sons down the dark dreary pit,
They'll be damned like the sinners in hell.

Anon.

Killed in Action

For N. J. de B.-L.
Crete, May, 1941

His chair at the table, empty,
His home clothes hanging in rows forlorn,
His cricket bat and cap, his riding cane,
The new flannel suit he had not worn.
His dogs, restless, with tortured ears
Listening for his swift, light tread upon the path.
And there – his violin! Oh his violin! Hush! hold your tears.

Juliette de Bairacli-Levy

Dear Yuri

Dear Yuri, I remember you,
the man with the funny name
who the Russians sent into space,
were you desperate for fame?

There surely must have been safer ways
to get into the history books,
perhaps you couldn't rock like Elvis
or you hadn't got James Dean's looks.

Perhaps you couldn't fight like Ali
or make a political speech
so they packed you into a spaceship
and sent you out of Earth's reach.

And, Yuri, what was it like
to be way out there in space,
the first to break free of Earth's gravity
and look down on the human race?

I'd been doing my maths all morning
and at lunchtime I heard what you'd done.
I told everyone back at school
How you'd rocketed near to the sun.

And, Yuri, I wanted to say
that I remember your flight,
I remember your name, Gagarin,
And the newsreel pictures that night.

And you must have pep talked like others
when they took off into the blue.
I've forgotten their names, but, Yuri,
I'll always remember you.

Brian Moses

R

Rescuing the
World

Hurt No Living Thing

Hurt no living thing,
Ladybird nor butterfly,
Nor moth with dusty wing,
Nor cricket chirping cheerily,
Nor grasshopper, so light of leap,
Nor dancing gnat,
Nor beetle fat,
Nor harmless worms that creep.

Christina Rossetti

An Alphabet for the Planet

A for air.
The gentle breeze by which we live.
B for bread.
A food to bake, and take – and *give*.
C for climate.
It can be warm, it can be cold . . .
D for dolphin.
A smiling friend no net should hold.
E for Earth.
Our ship through space, and home to share.
F for family.
Which also means people *everywhere*.
G for green.
Colour of life we'll help to spread.
H for healthy.
Happy and strong, no fumes with lead.
I for ivory.
The elephant's tusks, his *own* to keep.
J for jungle.
A rainforest. No axe should creep.
K for kindly.
To everyone, gentle and good.
L for life.
It fills the sea and town and wood.
M for mother.
She may feel hurt, but loves us all.
N for nest.
A tiny home for chicks so small.

O for Ozone.
It shields our Earth from harmful rays.
P for peace.
'My happy dream,' the Planet says.
Q for quiet.
Where no loud noise can get at you.
R for recycled.
Old cans and cards as good as new.
S for Sun.
The nearest star. It gives us light.
T for tree.
A grander plant, a green delight.
U for united.
Working as one to put things right.
V for victory.
Winning over disease and war.
W for water.
The whole earth drinks when rainclouds pour.
X for Xylophone.
Music from wood – the high notes soar!
Y for yummy.
Those tasty fruits 'organically grown'.
Z for zoo.
A cage, a condor – sad, alone.

Riad Nourallah

On the Third Day

And the carpenter said, 'I shall make a machine
that will filter the air clean of its poison;
that will pump and drag up water
from the deep rocks to the sky; a guardian of rainbows,
that will hold the soil steady, knotting it tight
with invisible, intricate webbing.
A machine that will surfeit a million insects,
hold the birds and the climbing tribes of apes;
a protection for my sons against wind and lightning,
a fuel that will heat their hands and faces;
whose by-products will be ships, and violins, and gallows;
whose shavings will be stained with my children's names,
their truths slowly discovered, their gorgeous lies,
their fingers' deftness with blue and gold and ochre.
My machine will cause poets to make verse,
will smell like honey and rain and ashes;
will break out yearly in a rash of apples;
will unleash a million berries.
I will call it oak, and beech and thorn;
I will design it in a thousand shapes and places,
and I will give it to my sons for their salvation
– let them guard it well.

On the day the sun dies and the rain is bitter
I will come and hang my sorrows from its branches.'

Catherine Fisher

Our Tree

It takes so long for a tree to grow
So many years of pushing the sky.

Long branches stretch their arms
Reach out with their wooden fingers.

Years drift by, fall like leaves
From green to yellow then back to green.

Since my Grandad was a boy
And then before his father's father

There's been an elm outside our school
Its shadow long across our playground.

Today three men ripped it down.
Chopped it up. It took ten minutes.

David Harmer

The Rainbow Mystery

One minute it was raining,
the sun had just peeked through,
and all things were as normal
when out of the grey and blue

this great big coloured arch
leapt into the sky
several miles wide, I guess,
and pretty near as high

and stood without permission,
over council land,
an unofficial structure
of the kind that we had banned.

No one had sought approval
or put in an application,
it was clearly a cowboy job
with ideas above its station.

And then it went clean missing
leaving nothing in its place
and the company that built it
is proving hard to trace.

George Szirtes

Changes

My butterfly brooch is flitting off
Through the open window;
The hedgehog from the hearthstone moved
Sure though slow;
The bird in the picture on the tree
Has gone, and the real sea
Must have taken back the crabs and shells
We put in the pebble-filled watery jars.

Where, you ask, have our creatures gone?
They moved away when you left home.

Jenny Joseph

Scarecrow Christmas

In winter fields
a scarecrow sings
the hopeful tune
of lonely kings.

His empty heart
is thin and cold.
His cruel rags
are worn and old.

350

But in our homes
we sing out clear,
warm words of joy
and know no fear.

In bed at night
we listen for
padded footsteps
at the door.

In other fields
and different lands,
living scarecrows
reach out hands.

They live beneath
the sun's cruel rays.
They do not know
of Christmas days.

Pie Corbett

The Last Bear

The last bear left, the last bear left,
The last bear left, that's me –
No other bears in all the world
To keep me company.

I climb the hills of summer,
I wade the empty streams,
I fatten up in autumn,
Winter's a cave of dreams.

My dreams are full of playing
And tumbling in a heap
With twenty other happy bears,
But then I wake from sleep,

And yawn and stretch and scratch
And search the woods once more –
No bear-scent on the north wind,
No trace of pad or paw.

The last bear left, the last bear left,
The last bear left, that's me –
No other bears in all the world
To keep me company.

Richard Edwards

Proverbial Logic

Where there are pandas
there's bamboo, but the converse
is sadly not true.

Debjani Chatterjee

The Cabbage White Butterfly

I look like a flower you could pick. My delicate wings
Flutter over the cabbages. I don't make
Any noise ever. I'm among the silent things.
   Also I easily break.

I have seen the nets in your hands. At first I thought
A cloud had come down but then I noticed you
With your large pink hand and arm. I was nearly caught
   But fortunately I flew

Away in time, hid while you searched, then took
To the sky, was out of your reach. Like a nameless flower
I tried to appear. Can't you be happy to look?
   Must you possess with your power?

Elizabeth Jennings

Missing

Missing: our
one and only planet,
known to her friends as
'Earth'.

Yes, an old photograph
when she was clothed in
gorgeous greens,
wilderness white,
brilliant blues.

Somehow, got into
bad company:
blistered brown,
gaunt grey,
faded. Jaded,

left one morning;
no forwarding address.

We just didn't think . . .
We just didn't think . . .
what to do.

If you
have any information
that can help us trace
our beautiful planet,
please get in touch.

Please get in touch.

Mike Johnson

To Mother Earth

The land is black
The seas are brown
I'm sorry
That we let you down

Roger Stevens

Prayer for Earth

Last night
an owl
called from the hill.
Coyotes howled.
A deer stood still
nibbling at bushes far away.
The moon shone silver.
Let this stay.

Today
two noisy crows
flew by,
their shadows pasted to the sky.
The sun broke out
through clouds of grey.
An iris opened.
Let this stay.

Myra Cohn Livingston

My Moccasins Have Not Walked

My moccasins have not walked
Among the giant forest trees

My leggings have not brushed
Against the fern and berry bush

My medicine pouch has not been filled
with roots and herbs and sweetgrass

My hands have not fondled the spotted fawn

My eyes have not beheld
The golden rainbow of the north

My hair has not been adorned
With the eagle feather

Yet
My dreams are dreams of these
My heart is one with them
The scent of them caresses my soul

Duke Redbird

from *Auguries of Innocence*

To see a World in a Grain of Sand
And a Heaven in a Wild Flower,
Hold Infinity in the palm of your hand
And Eternity in an hour.

William Blake

S

Senses and Feelings

The Oldest Girl in the World

Children, I remember how I could hear
with my soft young ears
the tiny sounds of the air –
tinkles and chimes
like minuscule bells
ringing continually there;
clinks and chinks
like glasses of sparky gooseberry wine,
jolly and glinting and raised in the air.
Yes, I could hear like a bat. And how!
Can't hear a sniff of it now.

Truly, believe me, I could all the time see
every insect that crawled in a bush,
every bird that hid in a tree,
individually.
If I wanted to catch a caterpillar
to keep as a pet in a box
I had only to watch a cabbage
And there it would be
Crawling bendy and green towards me.
Yes, I could see with the eyes of a cat. Miaow!
Can't see a sniff of it now.

And my sense of taste was second to none,
By God, the amount I knew with my tongue!
The shrewd taste of a walnut's brain.
The taste of a train from a bridge.
Of a kiss. Of air chewy with midge.
Of fudge from a factory two miles away
from the house where I lived.
I'd stick out my tongue
to savour these in a droplet of rain.
Yes, I could taste like the fang of a snake. Wow!
Can't taste a sniff of it now.

On the scent, what couldn't I smell
with my delicate nose, my nostrils of pearl?
I could smell the world!
Snow. Soot. Soil.
Satsumas snug in their Christmas sock.
The ink of a pen.
The stink of an elephant's skin.
The blue broth of a swimming pool. Dive in!
The showbizzy gasp of the wind.
Yes, I could smell like a copper's dog, Bow-wow!
Can't smell a sniff of it now.

As for my sense of touch
it was too much!
The cold of a snowball
felt through the vanishing heat of a mitt.
A peach like an apple wearing a vest.
The empty dish of a bird's nest.
A hot chestnut
branding the palm at the heart of the fist.
The stab of the thorn on the rose. Long grass, its itch.
Yes, I could feel with the sensitive hand of a ghost. Whooo!
Can't feel a sniff of it now.

Can't see a
Can't hear a
Can't taste a
Can't smell a
Can't feel a bit of it whiff of it sniff of it.
Can't get a sniff of it now.

Carol Ann Duffy

The Magic of the Brain

Such a sight I saw:
An eight-sided kite surging up into a cloud
Its eight tails streaming out as if they were one.
It lifted my heart as starlight lifts the head
Such a sight I saw.

And such a sound I heard.
One bird through dim winter light as the day was closing
Poured out a song suddenly from an empty tree.
It cleared my head as water refreshes the skin
Such a sound I heard.

Such a smell I smelled:
A mixture of roses and coffee, of green leaf and warmth
It took me to gardens and summer and cities abroad,
Memories of meetings as if my past friends were here
Such a smell I smelled.

Such soft fur I felt.
It wrapped me around, soothing my winter-cracked skin,
Not gritty or stringy or sweaty but silkily warm
As my animal slept on my lap, and we both breathed content
Such soft fur I felt.

Such food I tasted:
Smooth-on-tongue soup, and juicy crackling of meat,
Greens like fresh fields, sweet-on-your palate peas,
Jellies and puddings with fragrance of fruit they are made from
Such good food I tasted.

Such a world comes in:
Far world of the sky to breathe in through your nose
Near world you feel underfoot as you walk on the land.
Through your eyes and your ears and your mouth and your
   brilliant brain
Such a world comes in.

Jenny Joseph

The First Bit

I love the first bit of the morning,
The bit of the day that no one has used yet,
The part that is so clean
You must wipe your feet before you walk out into it.
The bit that smells like rose petals and cut grass
And dampens your clothes with dew.

If you go out you will bump into secrets,
Discover miracles usually covered by bus fumes.
You will hear pure echoes, whispers and scuttling.

I love the first bit of the morning
When the sun has only one eye open
And the day is like a clean shirt,
Uncreased and ready to put on;
The part that gets your attention
By being so quiet.

Coral Rumble

By the River

Lying on the river bank
beneath the trailing willow,
my anorak behind my head
folded as a pillow,

I close my eyes and listen to
the many sounds around me,
lapping water near my feet,
a mumbling, fumbling brown bee,

a jenny wren in the branches
twitching among the twigs,
a grasshopper not far away
scratching itchy legs,

a coo-coo-cooing pigeon
high up in an old oak tree,
like someone sawing a plank of wood –
and sawing endlessly!

A breeze is whiffling through the grass
like a comb running through your hair,
and little-globs-of-amber-ants
are scuttering here and there.

The river's sliding gently,
dreaming of the sea,
and I am thinking of only one thing:
strawberries and cream for tea!

Matt Simpson

Allotment

All day, nobody clanged the latch
of the wooden five-bar gate;
all day, the cabbage whites surfed randomly
through the tents of runner beans,
and dahlias nodded red and heavy-headed.
Stupefied by solitude and the sun I stared
at the spade and the baked clay
from the shade of an apple tree,
where I ate three apples.

Judith Green

The Wild Cat

Lies, cryptic in heather
Or warms flanks on noon-hot rock;
Is not asleep,
Senses with closed eyes
The careless wren – a mouthful;
Listens to the lark,
At the same time hears the beetle;
Waits the long-shadowed afternoon
And rabbits.
Moves in shadow
Is shadow.
Flows, melts into night.
The moon stage-lights the mouse.

Catherine Benson

Me and the Moon

It stopped me dead in my tracks,
as I was going home,
late one afternoon –

A sudden orange moon
floating above the trees
like a big night-time balloon.

Sky-struck, I gazed up.
Was it the moon?
Or was it the sun?

A sunset sun
some great big hand
had tossed back up again?

Now I'm running, heart thudding,
angels at my heels,
resurrection trumpets.

Back home, I stare up through the window,
clasping my clammy seven-year-old hands:
'Please God, don't make the world end, not yet.'

Then I hear my mother's voice behind me,
catching me in its net of safety,
bouncing me right back to right.

'What a beautiful big full moon tonight.'

Grace Nichols

In the crisp-packet

In the crisp-packet
a blue paper twist of salt:
the night sky, the stars.

Richard Leigh

Another Sensational Day

The roar of parents,
A curse of clocks;
Tinkle of toilets,
Shrugging on socks.

The flop of cereal,
Pop song of toast;
Hurdling buses,
The bell's mad boast.

The jam of lessons,
As hours overtake;
The theft of daydreams,
The scent of break.

A rush-hour of shoes,
The dawdle of light,
A gaggle of gossip
Summoning night.

Excuses for homework,
The glue of the box,
A sinking of pillows . . .

The curse of clocks.

Andrew Fusek Peters

Mood Manager

Come on LAZY MOOD
let me stay in bed
all day, reading and eating.

Come on SCARY MOOD
see a monster make me scream
something truly awful.

Come on BIG BOLD MOOD
make me beat up
a pensioner's burglar.

Come on SAD MOOD
stop saying remember:
Grandma is dead for ever.

Come on WILLING MOOD
have me pushing home
a weary wheelchair person.

Come on MEAN MISERY MOOD
make me manage without
touching my pocket money.

Come on GUESSING MOOD
make me guess my wished-for
birthday gift, there parcelled up.

Come on TICKLED MOOD
keep me feeling trumps
answering that quiz correctly.

Come on LUCKY MOOD
make it a lottery win
houseful of money today.

Come on NOISY MOOD
make me holler, shouting:
I passed the test!

James Berry

It's Not What I'm Used To

I don't want to go to Juniors . . .

The chairs are too big.
I like my chair small, so I fit
Exactly
And my knees go
Just so
Under the table.

And that's another thing –
The tables are too big.
I like my table to be
Right
For me
So my workbook opens
Properly.
And my pencil lies in the space at the top
The way my thin cat stretches into a long line
On the hearth at home.

Pencils – there's another other thing.
Another problem.
Up in Juniors they use pens and ink.
I shall really have to think

About ink.

Jan Dean

The World Is Dark When All My Friends Grow Cold

The world is dark when all my friends grow cold,
And icy stares show no sign of a thaw,
And even Ben believes the lies he's told.

The gossip is protected like it's gold
And each will add to it a little more;
The world is dark when all my friends grow cold.

The hurtful lies soon grow a hundredfold.
I hear my name when passing by each door,
And even Ben believes the lies he's told.

Now all the fragile memories I hold
Of loyal friends are broken on the floor;
The world is dark when my friends grow cold.

I realize my secrets have been sold,
My heart is rubbed with sadness till it's raw.
And even Ben believes the lies he's told.

Mum says that I must learn to be more bold,
Dad says life's tough, I have to know the score;
The world is dark when my friends grow cold.
And even Ben believes the lies he's told.

Coral Rumble

Cornered

They chased me to the corner of the playground,
Where the air is colder
Because spiteful gusts of wind rush at the chain-link fence,
And dust blows in your face, rubs like sandpaper.

One tear escaped – then all was lost.
In for the kill, their teeth flashed through parted lips,
Their eyes narrowed in contempt.
I stared at the tarmac, cornered.

Rhymed insults sang a sneering song around my head
And, 'Baby! Baby! Baby!' boxed my ears
Until I was on the ground
My fingers spread over my face like prison bars.

Coral Rumble

Death Slide

Frozen with fear
I stood at the top,
staring down
at the vertical drop.

My father's voice echoed in my head:
'Be brave, be tough,' he'd always said.

Thirty feet high.
They call it 'Death Slide'.
They said I'd miss out
if I didn't ride.

My father's voice echoed in my head:
'Don't be a coward,' he'd always said.

Pairs of eyes all watch,
waiting for me to go.
It seemed like a lifetime passed
until finally I said, 'No!'

Now there's another voice in my head:
'You're the one who's brave,' it said.

Tracey Blance

in the dentist's waiting room

In the dentist's waiting room
tulips with their petals
tightly shut

George Swede

World Book Day Blues

Playtime.
Cinderella munches crisps.
Tinkerbell loses her hairband.
A worried teacher separates a sword-fighting duo.
A ghost trips over his sheet.
I hide in a quiet corner.
Why am I the only one not dressed up?

Catherine Glew
(11 years old)

The Luck of Life

There was a lucky boy
And he lived in a house.
His room was painted silver
The door: brown and green.

There was a lucky fox
And he lived in a wood,
Just on the edge of it
In a sandy bank under trees.

There was a lucky rat
And he lived in a pipe
Half buried in a building
In the middle of a town.

There was a lucky snake
In a biscuit-yellow place.
Miles and miles it stretched
With rocks for shade to sleep in.

All these things were charmed.
Their luck was the air they breathed.
They lived sometimes in danger,
Sometimes they played in peace.
They slept or they scurried,
They moved and breathed and ate.
There was colour in their houses
And firm earth underneath.

Jenny Joseph

Give Yourself a Hug

Give yourself a hug
when you feel unloved

Give yourself a hug
when people put on airs
to make you feel a bug

Give yourself a hug
when everyone seems to give you
a cold-shoulder shrug

Give yourself a hug –
a big big hug

And keep on singing,
'Only one in a million like me
Only one in a million-billion-
    trillion-zillion
like me.'

Grace Nichols

T
Teachers

The Horrible Headmonster

A new Headmaster arrives next week
  and rumours about him are rife.
They say he growls like a grizzly bear
  and that he chopped up his wife.

It's said he'll stride and stomp around the school
  like a zombie in the night,
and that his icicle stare can freeze
  hundreds of children with fright.

It's rumoured he wears a skull-shaped ring,
  and a tie with nests of fleas.
When he smiles he shows razor-sharp fangs.
  There are tattoos on his knees.

We've heard that he has a werewolf's howl.
There's a jagged scar on his cheek.
They say that he owns a whippy cane
  and that he'll use it next week.

Already he's called the 'The Headmonster'
  and some have named him 'The Ghoul'.
We'll soon find out if the rumours are true
  when he arrives at our school.

Wes Magee

The I-Spy Book of Teachers

One point if you catch your teacher yawning.
Double that to two if later on you find her snoring.
Three points if you hear your teacher singing
and four if it's a pop song not a hymn.
A generous five points if you ever see them jogging
and six if you should chance upon them snogging.
Seven if you ever find her on her knees and praying
for relief from noisy boys who trouble her.
Eight if you should catch him in the betting shop,
nine if you see him dancing on Top of the Pops.
And ten if you hear her say what a lovely class she's got
for then you'll know there's something
      quite seriously wrong with her.

Brian Moses

Where Do All the Teachers Go?

Where do all the teachers go
When it's 4 o'clock?
Do they live in houses
And do they wash their socks?

Do they wear pyjamas
And do they watch TV?
And do they pick their noses
The same as you and me?

Do they live with other people
Have they mums and dads?
And were they ever children
And were they ever bad?

Did they ever, never spell right
Did they ever make mistakes?
Were they punished in the corner
If they pinched the chocolate flakes?

Did they ever lose their hymn books
Did they ever leave their greens?
Did they scribble on the desk tops
Did they wear old dirty jeans?

I'll follow one back home today
I'll find out what they do
Then I'll put it in a poem
That they can read to you.

Peter Dixon

How Teachers Leave School Each Evening

The dance teacher floats down the stairway
and waltzes herself to the door.
Behind her the maths teacher counts every step
as he paces across the floor.

The geography teacher struggles to find
a different route home each night.
The PE teacher sets new daily records
for the swiftest homeward flight.

The English teacher recites to himself
lines of poetry of Keats.
The drama teacher's on camera,
a movie star in the streets.

The RE teacher prays
that there'll be no traffic queues.
The physics teacher knows there will
and regularly blows a fuse.

The IT teacher imagines he's left
as he follows some virtual route on screen.
It's a mystery why the history teacher
is met each night by a limousine.

Our music teacher, an Elvis freak,
plays air guitar along the drive,
with his rocker's quiff and Las Vegas suit
he's out there (somewhere) perfecting his jive.

But the teacher who's young and still keen
reluctantly closes the door,
ticks off the hours and minutes till she can be
back with her class once more.

Brian Moses

Practical Science

Do you remember 'Science',
    with weird Mr McPhee,
        who said, 'My boomerang's
        amazing: throw it, curves
            back, catch it, watch
                and see.' Threw it, curved
                back, caught it. 'Easy-
                peasy as can be.'
        Threw it, curved back,
    turned to answer me . . .
Woke up in *Casualty*.

Mike Johnson

Sir's a Secret Agent

Sir's a secret agent
He's licensed to thrill
At Double-Oh Sevening
He's got bags of skill.

He's tall, dark and handsome
With a muscular frame
Teaching's his profession
But Danger's his game!

He's cool and he's calm
When he makes a decision
He's a pilot, sky-diver
And can teach long-division.

No mission's too big
No mission's too small
School-kids, mad scientists
He takes care of them all.

He sorts out the villains
The spies and the crooks
Then comes back to school
And marks all our books!

Tony Langham

Fishy Stories

There was a bright teacher from Torquay
who went to fight sharks in the North Sea.
When asked why he had,
he said ''Cos I'm mad
And it's safer than teaching 4c.'

Dave Calder

The Excuse

She walked in nervously, biting her lip;
Trembling slightly, she could not meet their gaze.
'WELL?' shouted the class together –
Startled, the teacher made for the desk where
Behind the relative security of four wooden legs and
A jar of fading daisies
She felt an explanation coming on.
'WHERE'S OUR HOMEWORK?' yelled the class.
'Erm, well,' said the teacher, 'I haven't got it with me.'
'A LIKELY STORY,' sneered the class.
'YOU HAVEN'T DONE IT, HAVE YOU?' chorused the
    class.
'YOU HAVEN'T EVEN BOTHERED TO MARK OUR
    HOMEWORK!' they cried.
Inside her head she scrabbled desperately for something
    believable,

Sweat tricking down her temple and inside her palms.
'I dropped it getting off the bus. It landed
In a puddle then a
Huge gang of teachers took if off me and said
I wouldn't be let into the Staffroom Coffee-Tea Rotation
  Posse if I did it.
"Marking homework is for wimps," they said,' she said
  sadly,
A big round tear rolling slowly down her cheek.
'OH,' said the class, shifting uncomfortably,
'WELL, JUST MAKE SURE YOU HAVE IT FOR
  TOMORROW.
THERE, THERE, NO NEED TO CRY.'
'Thank you, class,' sniffed the teacher, brightening a little.
'It won't happen again, I promise.'

Jane Wright

The Prime Minister Is Ten Today

This morning I abolished
homework, detention and dinner ladies.
I outlawed lumpy custard, school mashed spuds
and handwriting lessons.
From now on play-times must last two hours
unless it rains, in which case we all go home
except the teachers who must do extra PE
outside in the downpour.

Whispering behind your hand in class
must happen each morning between ten and twelve,
and each child needs only do
ten minutes' work in one school hour.

I've passed a No Grumpy Teacher law
so one bad word or dismal frown
from Mr Spite or Miss Hatchetface
will get them each a month's stretch
sharpening pencils and marking books
inside the gaol of their choice.

All headteachers are forbidden
from wearing soft soled shoes
instead they must wear wooden clogs
so you can hear them coming.
They are also banned from shouting
or spoiling our assembly by pointing
at the ones who never listen.

Finally the school must shut
for at least half the year
and if the weather's really sunny
the teachers have to take us all
to the seaside for the day.

If you've got some good ideas
for other laws about the grown-ups
drop me a line in Downing Street
I'll always be glad to listen
come on, help me change a thing or two
before we all grow up
and get boring.

David Harmer

Staff Meeting

The teachers have gathered in private to talk
About their collections of left-over chalk –
Bits that are rare, bits they just like,
And fragments they've saved just in case there's a strike.
One has a blue that you don't often see,
Another a remnant from nineteen-oh-three.

They've thousands of pieces in boxes and tins,
Each sorted and counted with tweezers and pins.
And when all their best bits have been on display,
They'll take them home carefully, and lock them away.

Nick Toczek

We Lost Our Teacher to the Sea

We've been at the seaside all day
collecting shells, drawing the view,
doing science in the rockpools.

Our teacher went out to find the sea's edge,
and stayed there, he's sitting on a rock
he won't come back.

His glasses are frosted over with salt,
his beard has knotted into seaweed,
his black suit is covered in limpets.

He is staring into the wild water
singing to the waves,
sharing a joke with the herring gulls.

We sent out the coastguard,
the lifeboat and the orange helicopter;
he told them all to go away.

We're getting on the bus with our sticks of rock
our presents for Mum
and our jotters and pencils.

He's still out there as we leave,
arms outstretched to the pale blue sky
the tide racing towards him.

His slippery fishtail flaps,
with a flick and a shimmer he's gone
back to the sea forever.

David Harmer

The Pencil Stub

For William Penn School, Stoke Newington

When I was new I drew
the leather shoe lace on a magic shoe.

You shaved me down.

I wound my lead around
the leaves of an ancient
willow tree.

You shaved me down.

I drew a circle, you
rubbed me out,
I became a careful square.

You shaved me down.

I was happiest tracing
the face of your mother –
her plaited hair,
her sparkling slate grey eyes.

And still you shaved me down.

I could still conjure the universe,
skirt Saturn with a silver ring,
chase the rain falling from
a shooting star.

Chrissie Gittins

The Interesting Table

There's a table which stands at the end of the class
With interesting things galore
If it's weird or curious
That's where it goes
It's what 'Interesting Tables' are for.

There's an adder's skin, mandolin, thingummyjig
From whatshisname's big sister's house;
A ball signed by Wigan Athletic
And a nit comb with one half-squashed louse.

When we bring something in we discuss it
Then write a poem or two
Miss Bell says it helps to imagine
What interesting objects might feel, say or do.

One day Justin Smethwick turned up with a bag
And a mischievous smile on his face
Then up to the table he boldly went
Put his interesting thing in pride of place.

It was . . .

A TOMATO

'Really interesting, Justin!' the class all jeered
Miss Bell's bottom lip hit the floor
And she ushered him out of the classroom
To the interesting corridor.

Lindsay MacRae

Reading Round the Class

On Friday we have reading round the class.
Kimberley Bloomer is the best.
She sails slowly along the page like a great galleon
And everyone looks up and listens.
'Beautiful reading, Kimberley, dear,' sighs Mrs Scott,
'And with such fluency, such feeling.
It's a delight to hear.'

On Friday we have reading round the class.
I'm the worst.
I stumble and mumble along slowly like a broken-down
    train
And everyone looks up and listens.
Then they smile and snigger and whisper behind their
    hands.
'Dear me,' sighs Mrs Scott, 'rather rusty, Simon.
Quite a bit of practice needed, don't you think?
Too much television and football, that's your trouble,
And not enough reading.'

And she wonders why I don't like books.

Gervase Phinn

The Music Lesson Rap

I'm the bongo kid,
I'm the big-drum-beater,
I'm the click-your-sticks,
I'm the tap-your-feeter.
When the lesson starts,
When we clap our hands,
Then it's me who dreams
Of the boom-boom bands,
And it's me who stamps,
And it's me who yells
For the biff-bang gong,
Or the ding-dong bells,
Or the cymbals (large),
Or the cymbals (small),
Or the tubes that chime
Round the bash-crash hall,
Or the tambourine,
Or the thunder-maker –
But all you give me
Is the sssh-sssh shaker!

Clare Bevan

Football in the Rain

It's drizzling.
'Football practice!'
'Oh, sir!
Do we have to?'
We look hopefully at Mr Tomkins,
But he says,
'Don't be such babies!'
So out we go.

It's raining harder.
We all start to moan,
'Can't we go in, sir?
We're getting soaked!'
But Mr Tomkins is not impressed.
'Tough. Get on with it!'
He says, putting up his umbrella
And retreating to the touchline.

It's coming down in buckets.
There are puddles all over the pitch,
And the rest is just mud.
Eddy falls over,
And comes up looking like
The Mud Monster from Hell.
We all start falling over,
Because we all want to look like that.

It's really chucking it down.
Mr Tomkins gets rain in his whistle.
Gurgle-gurgle-PHEEEP!
'Everybody in!'
We start moaning again.
'Oh, sir!
Do we have to?'

David Orme

The Bubble Between Two Buildings

Wet petals stick ragged pink splodges
onto the path
         that twists and wriggles
under my feet like a long black snake.

The wind is warm, I can smell
blossom as it bends on its branches
watch it fly
         in a shower of flowers
scattered into the rain spattering down.

I'm stuck in a bubble between two buildings
my arms full of registers, messages, parcels
all the classrooms
              buzz like beehives full of bustle
children and grown-ups all painting and writing
talking and thinking, laughing and singing
chattering, shouting, counting and weighing.

Outside I can hear
the milk float droning down our street
the other side of the fence
              two dogs barking
and birds singing in the hedge by the path.

It's still and calm
breathing the blossom-heavy air
I lean into the warm, wet wind
              wait for my feet
to lead me back to my busy classroom
down the shining tarmac painted with blossom.

David Harmer

The Last Day of the School Holiday

The Geography teacher had a faraway look
The History teacher forgot what day it was
The RE teacher was having doubts
The Cookery teacher's mind was scrambled
The Science teacher could see the gravity of the situation
The Art teacher was drawing the wrong conclusion
The PE teacher was trying to jog her memory
The Maths teacher was feeling negative
The Woodwork teacher was pining away
The Music teacher was playing up
The English teacher couldn't comprehend it
The French teacher was using bad language

And the Head ached

Mike Jubb

U

Unpleasant Things

January 7

My father left us in the dead of winter.
Snow shut the door. Snow turned the key.
My father left us in the dead of winter.
Now I leave blank the pages of my diary.

Stephen Knight

The Shoes

These are the shoes
Dad walked about in
when we did jobs
in the garden,
when his shed
was full of shavings,
when he tried to put the fence up,
when my old bike
needed mending,
when the car
could not get started,
when he got up late
on Sunday.
These are the shoes
Dad walked about in
and I've kept them
in my room.

These are not the shoes
that Dad walked out in
when we didn't know
where he was going,
when I tried to lift
his suitcase,
when he said goodbye
and kissed me,
when he left his door-key
on the table,
when he promised Mum
he'd send a postcard,
when I couldn't hear
his special footsteps.
These are not the shoes
that Dad walked out in
but he'll need them
when he comes home.

John Mole

Nettles

My son aged three fell in the nettle bed.
'Bed' seemed a curious name for those green spears,
That regiment of spite behind the shed:
It was no place for rest. With sobs and tears
The boy came seeking comfort and I saw
White blisters beaded on his tender skin.
We soothed him till his pain was not so raw.
At last he offered us a watery grin,
And then I took my hook and honed the blade
And went outside and slashed in fury with it
Till not a nettle in that fierce parade
Stood upright any more. Next task: I lit
A funeral pyre to burn the fallen dead.
But in two weeks the busy sun and rain
Had called up tall recruits behind the shed:
My son would often feel sharp wounds again.

Vernon Scannell

Incendiary

That one small boy with a face like pallid cheese
And burnt-out little eyes could make a blaze
As brazen, fierce and huge, as red and gold
And zany yellow as the one that spoiled
Three thousand guineas' worth of property
And crops at Godwin's Farm on Saturday
Is frightening – as fact and metaphor:
An ordinary match intended for
The lighting of a pipe or kitchen fire
Misused may set a whole menagerie
Of flame-fanged tigers roaring hungrily.
And frightening, too, that one small boy should set
The sky on fire and choke the stars to heat
Such skinny limbs and such a little heart
Which would have been content with one warm kiss
Had there been anyone to offer this.

Vernon Scannell

The Purse

I pinched it from my mother's purse,
Pretending it's a game.
My muscles tightened: hard and tense.
I pinched it just the same.

'I need it as a loan,' I said.
'It's not against the law.'
'I won't do it again,' I said.
I've said all that before.

The reason was the cash at first,
It isn't any more;
I do it . . . well . . . because I do,
I don't know what it's for.

I only know that when the house
Is silent, empty, still,
I head towards my parents' room
As if against my will.

The sweat is cold upon my neck,
My back and arms feel strange,
I'm sure that someone's watching me
As I pick out her change.

But no one ever catches me,
Sometimes I wish they would;
Then perhaps I'd stop and think
And give it up for good.

But my mum trusts me, buys me things:
Each kindness makes it worse
Because I know, when she's next door
My hands will find her purse.

David Kitchen

The Spell

I've written a spell out on paper,
I've hidden the spell in a matchbox,
I've buried the spell in the garden,
I'm waiting for it to work.

*

The Beast didn't hit me this morning,
The Beast didn't hit me at lunch-time,
The Beast didn't hit me till swimming,
The spell is beginning to work.

*

The Beast wasn't there in assembly,
He's been in an accident, Dawn said,
I spent all of break in the playground,
The spell's going on with its work.

*

This morning they put up a notice,
He's broken his leg in three places,
I'm sorry. I'm not really sorry.
The spell has completed its work.

*

I've dug up the spell from the garden,
The writing's still clear on the paper,
I'm keeping it safe in its matchbox,
Just in case.

Richard Edwards

Me Missing A Party

I was on my way to a party.

It was just the usual crowded tube platform –
wind like a hairdryer full on
and a train coming.

the girl beside me twisted in slow motion
from the keyboard of the chocolate machine
her skirt blew out and blew in –

they said she was catching the tube home
after two hours' overtime,

she wasn't going to the party
but she got written into the story.

I wasn't really watching her.
I was playing with the thought of a Wispa
but my mind was elsewhere.

And when you heard the explosion
what did you feel? Did you run?

I never heard the explosion.
I was thinking of the party
when someone picked me up and threw me.

U – Unpleasant Things

The thing was, I couldn't get my breath.
My face was in something red.

But when you knew it was a bomb
was there much panic? Did you hear screaming
or did people stay calm?

The train must've come in
but the doors didn't open.

They must've missed it by a minute
because it only took a minute

I had my face in something red
but it was the girl's leg.

The doors stayed shut, that was the strangest thing –
all those faces staring.

First reports suggest a small bomb
hidden behind the chocolate machine.

The rest is history
or me missing a party.

Helen Dunmore

The Fear

I am the footsteps that crackle on gravel
and the sudden chill that's hard to explain.
I am the figure seen flitting through doorways
and the noisy rattle of a loose windowpane.

I am the scream that wakes you at night
with the thought, was it real or a dream?
I am the quickening thud of your heart
and the feeling things aren't what they seem.

I am the slam of a door blown shut
when there isn't even a breeze
and the total and absolute clarity
that you just heard someone sneeze

I am the midnight visitor,
the knock when there's no one there.
I am the ceiling creaking
and the soft footfall on your stair.

I am the shadows that dance on your wall
and the phantoms that float through your head
and I am the fear that you fear each night
as you wriggle down deep in your bed.

Brian Moses

Lost, One Siamese Cat

Like a stripped-down
engine, all his
working parts
are visible.

He wears his skin
like a speed-skater's suit,
gazes out from
blackcurrant eyes.

His face is all
triangles, black patent
nose, ears like
corner flags.

His whiskers sprout
from peppered holes;
yawning, his tongue is
a curling flame.

The most elegant
of cats, he steps with
Nureyev grace, purrs like
a thunderbox.

He pours himself
like cream from
window sill to puddle
of sunlight.

He has a voice
of a banshee, answers to
Sam. If found, return
to Jones, number 76,

PLEASE.

Moira Andrew

Lost Kitty in New York City, $500 Reward

Nothing has been heard,
not a single word,
about the lost kitty
in New York City.
No word from the birds,
it's quite absurd.
The rats won't rat,
the mice said, 'Scat,
it's rat-a-tat-tat
if we find that cat.'

On Madison Square
she was nowhere,
Up the Empire State
it was too late.
Down on Forty-first
they feared the worst,
but on Forty-third
somebody heard
that after dark
in Central Park,
three blind mice
spotted her twice,
started a whisper,
a silver whisker
had now been found
on Lennon's ground.

And one of them swore
that the print of a paw
and tracks of blood
had been seen in mud
by the Hudson River –
it would make you
        shiver . . .

There's little pity
for any lost kitty
in New York City.

Pie Corbett and
Brian Moses

The Aquarium

'Roll up, now! Roll up!'
Called the man on the pier.
'Come, visit the MERMAID!
Last chance this year.'

I paid him my penny,
I tiptoed inside,
I thought he had tricked me,
I thought he had lied . . .

But there was the mermaid,
Alone in the pool,
Just like the pictures
I'd studied at school.

Her hair was as glossy
And golden and wet,
Her tail was as silver
As moonlight, and yet

Her song was the saddest
I ever had heard,
Her eyes were as dull
As a poor, captured bird.

I ran from the mermaid,
I ran from the pier,
But still, in my head,
It's her voice that I hear.

And still, in my dreams,
She is gazing at me
As I carry her gently
Back home to the sea.

Clare Bevan

Billy's Coming Back

Word is out on the street tonight,
Billy's coming back.

There's a sound outside of running feet,
somebody, somewhere's switched on the heat,
policemen are beating a swift retreat
now Billy's coming back.

Only last year he went away
everyone heaved a sigh,
now news is out, and the neighbourhood
is set to blow sky-high.

Words are heard in the staff room,
teachers' faces deepen with gloom,
can't shrug off this feeling of doom
now Billy's coming back.

It was wonderful when he upped and left,
a carnival feeling straightaway,
no looking over shoulders,
each day was a holiday.

And now like a bomb no one dares to defuse,
time ticks on while kids quake in their shoes
no winners here, you can only lose,
now Billy's coming back.

It's dog eat dog on the street tonight,
it's cat and mouse, Billy's looking for a fight,
so take my advice, keep well out of sight
now Billy's coming back.

Brian Moses

V

Viewpoints

Wizard and Witch

I am the egg, and I will imprison you.
   I am the bird, and I will thrust for life.

But I am a cage; I shall see you pine away.
   I am a feather, drawn out on the wind.

Now I'm black tar, and I will weigh
   you down.
   I will be sunshine, to melt you and
     run free.

I will be fog, to choke you and confuse.
   My rains will come, dissolving you to dew.

Ah, but my river will swallow your every drop.
   I am a fish, and I will leap your dams.

But not my fine net, to hold you alive
   or dead.
   See, as pearls I drop down through your mesh.

Pierced and necklaced I hold you on my thread.
   But I glance away from you in moonlight sparks.

My chimney will hold you and turn you to soot.
   My cold heart will freeze me and turn me to
     snowflakes.

My hands will pack you into a snowball.
But when you fling me I will scatter as birds do.

I am the egg, and I will imprison you.

David Duncombe and Berlie Doherty

Mysteries

Why do dogs bury bones?
Why do kids like mobile phones?
Why do cats knead their paws?
Why does grass grow out of doors?

Why do clouds disappear?
Why do Dads drink lukewarm beer?
Why do birds sing at dawn?
Why do babies get stillborn?

Why do stars shine at night?
Why is maths always right?
Why do toes grow so slow?
Why avoid the mistletoe?

Why do stories have to end?
Why do cuts always mend?
Why do plums have a stone?
Why do tramps stay all alone?

Why do bombers want to kill?
Why does fame cause such a thrill?
Why does cancer make us ill?
Why does time not keep still?

Why do robbers grab and smash?
Why do nappies cause a rash?
Why do mysteries mystify?
Are the answers camera shy?

Pie Corbett

Learning

Today I learned
how a spider
wraps its silk
around a fly,
makes the web bounce
with urgent tread –
forward, wrap and back
forward wrap and back.
I watched until
the fly was glued,
the spider still,
the web less taut.

Today I learned
the ringdove's call,
like morse code
from our rooftop,
cuk-cuk-coo –
two short one long.
He kept it up for
ten neck-jerking minutes –
cuk-cuk-coo,
then dripped away
without a backward glance.

Today I learned
that daisies smell
like stale milk.
I picked one,
crushed its hairy stalk
between my fingers
and the fatty stink
lingered rancid
on my skin.

Today I learned
that cats have
tongues like sandpaper.
This tabby gave me
friendly licks
that rasped my fingers,
sent the shivers
spiralling
around my spine.

Today I would have learned
a lot more
but I had to go
to school.

Barrie Wade

Notes in Class

'You are like a red, red rose,'
he told her in his note.

'You are like a slimy slug,'
were the cruel words she wrote.

'My heart is yours for ever,'
he penned, 'forever true.'

'I would rather wash the dishes,'
she replied, 'than be with you.'

'You smell of summer flowers,'
he wrote, 'full blown and sweet.'

She wrote, 'You pong of sweaty socks
and even sweatier feet.'

He scrawled, 'My heart has broken
into pieces. I may die!'

She replied, 'Well why tell me,
I won't pretend I'd cry.'

He typed, 'My love has turned to hate.
My heart is now of stone.'

She scribbled, 'That's just typical.
I might have known you'd moan.'

Marian Swinger

The Dark Avenger

for 2 voices

My dog is called The Dark Avenger.
Hello, I'm Cuddles.

She understands every word I say.
Woof?

Last night I took her for a walk.
Woof! Walkies! Let's go!

Cleverly, she kept three paces ahead.
I dragged him along behind me.

She paused at every danger, spying out the land.
I stopped at every lamp-post.

When the coast was clear, she sped on.
I slipped my lead and ran away.

Scenting danger, Avenger investigated.
I found some fresh chip papers in the bushes.

I followed, every sense alert.
*He blundered through the trees, shouting 'Oy, come 'ere!
  Where are you?'*

Something – maybe a sixth sense – told me to stop.
He tripped over me in the dark.

There was a pale menacing figure ahead of us.
Then I saw the white Scottie from next door.

Avenger sprang into battle, eager to defend her master.
Never could stand terriers!

They fought like tigers.
We scrapped like dogs.

Until the enemy was defeated.
Till Scottie's owner pulled him off – spoilsport!

Avenger gave a victory salute.
I rolled in the puddles.

And came to check I was all right.
I shook mud over him.

'Stop it, you stupid dog!'
He congratulated me.

Sometimes, even The Dark Avenger can go too far.
Woof!!

Trevor Millum

Tiger Eyes

Always, always, where she walked,
one left, one right, two tigers stalked.
Sleek and striped, they paced along,
bright and beautiful and strong.
The great heads swung, the wild eyes glowed,
she never feared the lonely road,
the jostling crowd, the bully's sneer
for she had tigers, always near.
As she walked, the grimy streets
echoed to their tiger feet,
slowly padding, menace filled,
prowling past where rubbish spilled,
where shops were closed and graffiti
replaced the flowers, grass and trees.
When jeered at by the local louts
she knew neither fear nor doubt
though most of them were twice her size.
She fixed them with her tiger eyes
and went unharmed, for as they stared,
they almost saw the tigers there,
a gleam of gold, a scrape of claw,
a hint, a whisper of a roar,
a shadow cast where no sun shone,
an image, fleeting, flickering, gone.
For always, always, as she walked,
one left, one right, two tigers stalked.

Marian Swinger

The Wolf's Wife Speaks

He was always out and about.
First on the block
To be up at the crack of dawn
Sniffing the morning air.

Of course,
Pork was his favourite.
I tell you, he would go a long way
For a nice bit of crackling,
Or to catch a tasty piglet or two.

But in the end
It all got too much –
All that huffing and puffing
Up and down the den,
Muttering in his sleep
That he would blow the house down!

Something was wrong,
I could tell –
Something had put his nose
Out of joint.

He'd come home full of bravado,
Swaggering into the den,
Flashing me that wolfish grin –
All teeth and tongue –
Then he'd set about boasting,
Full of big talk about
blowing up another building.
It cut no ice with me.

The tell-tale signs were there –
Some days he'd get back
covered in straw,
hardly able to draw breath.
What he'd been up to,
Lord alone knows . . .

Well it all came to a head,
When late one afternoon –
He shot back in,
With his fur singed.

I had to laugh –
He looked so funny,
Stood there with his bare bottom
Red as a radish.
Talk about coming home
With his tail between his legs!
Where he'd been – I can't imagine.
He never said.

He stays more at home now.
Well, he's prone to bronchitis –
This time of year you can hear him coming,
Poor old thing –
Wheezing and puffing,
Hardly able to draw breath.

We don't talk about it –
And he's right off pork!
If you ask me,
It's all been
a bit of a blow
To his ego.

Pie Corbett

The Magic Show

After a feast of sausage rolls,
Sandwiches of various meats,
Jewelled jellies, brimming bowls
Of chocolate ice and other treats,
We children played at Blind Man's Buff,
Hide-and-Seek, Pin-the-Tail-on-Ned,
And then – when we'd had just enough
Of party games – we all were led
Into another room to see
The Magic Show. The wizard held
A wand of polished ebony;
His white-gloved, flickering hands compelled
The rapt attention of us all.
He conjured from astonished air
A living pigeon and a fall
Of paper snowflakes; made us stare
Bewildered, as a playing card –
Unlike a leopard – changed its spots
And disappeared. He placed some starred
And satin scarves in silver pots,
Withdrew them as plain bits of rag,
Then swallowed them before our eyes.
But soon we felt attention flag
And found delighted, first surprise
Had withered like a wintry leaf;
And, when the tricks were over, we
Applauded, yet felt some relief,
And left the party willingly.

'Good night', we said, 'and thank you for
The lovely time we've had.' Outside
The freezing night was still. We saw
Above our heads the slow clouds stride
Across the vast, unswallowable skies;
White, graceful gestures of the moon,
The stars intent and glittering eyes,
And, gleaming like a silver spoon,
The frosty path to lead us home.
Our breath hung blossoms on unseen
Boughs of air as we passed there,
And we forgot that we had been
Pleased briefly by that conjuror,
Could not recall his tricks, or face,
Bewitched and awed, as now we were,
By magic of the commonplace.

Vernon Scannell

A Good Poem

I like a good poem.
One with lots of fighting
in it. Blood, and the
clanging of armour. Poems

against Scotland are good,
and poems that defeat
the French with crossbows.
I don't like poems that

aren't about anything.
Sonnets are wet and
a waste of time.
Also poems that don't

Know how to rhyme.
If I was a poem
I'd play football and
get picked for England.

Roger McGough

W

Wonder

The Shooting Stars

That night
we went out in the dark
and saw the shooting stars
was one of the best nights ever

It was as if someone
was throwing paint
across the universe

The stars just kept coming
and we 'oohed' and 'aahed'
like on bonfire night

And it didn't matter
they weren't real stars –
just bits of dust on fire
burning up in the atmosphere

And we stayed out there for ages
standing on this tiny planet
staring up at the vast cosmos

And I shivered
with the thrill
of it all

James Carter

Up on the Roof

Up on the roof of a church
was a small, blond boy
and a black and white kitten.

Down below, the priest
was praying aloud,
pleading with God,

asking him to keep
this small boy from falling
down from his church.

He couldn't phone the mother
as he didn't know her,
and cats all looked the same.

When the verger appeared
with a telescopic ladder
the priest closed his eyes

and, gripping his rosary,
he prayed in the dark until
the verger began to climb.

The boy was on his feet now
calling the kitten
who refused to move.

'Sit down,' begged the priest,
in an almost whisper
so as not to alarm the boy

who paid no attention,
walking over the slates
as if on the pavement

or as if he had wings –
with the sun in his hair
he looked like an angel.

When the verger's bald head
rose above the drainpipe
the boy had the kitten

and was walking back,
along the ridge,
with a beatific smile.

Matthew Sweeney

Playing with Stars

Young children know what it's like
to play with stars.

First of all it's a wink and a smile
from some distant constellation,
then it's hide and seek as they disappear
in a cover of cloud.
Sometimes children see how far
they can travel to a star
before familiar voices call them
home to bed.

Like all good games, of course,
you need to use a little imagination
when playing with stars.
More experienced players
can jump over stars
or shake down a star.
Some can trap them in butterfly nets,
but you should always let them loose again.
Stars grow pale and die if you cage them.

Sometimes the stars tell stories
of their journeys across the sky
and sometimes they stay silent.
At these times children may travel themselves,
wandering a line that unravels
through their dreams.
At those times too, the stars play their own games,
falling from the sky when there's no one there
to catch them.

Sometimes you find these stars on the ground,
dazed and confused. Be warned though,
even fallen stars may be hot to touch.

Young children know what it's like
to rescue stars, to hold them gently
in gloved hands and then,
with one almighty fling
sling them back to the sky.

Adults forget what it's like
to play with stars
and when children offer to teach them
they're far too busy.

Brian Moses

White Horse

As a child I dreamt
a white horse would come
and carry me away.
Not that my childhood was unhappy,
it was just that my small boy head
was full of adventures.
The horse was a noble beast,
perhaps a unicorn
in a previous existence,
an elemental creature
of ice and fire
with a mane like a shower of stars.

I believed I had only to wish for the horse
and we'd flee over fields
to the sea, or rescue princesses
with long-flowing tresses
before galloping a path to the clouds.
And there were those moments
when the sky conjured up
a rainbow bridge,
where we may have passed
from this world to another.

Later I discovered
that the white horse
wasn't rooted in childhood.
I came to realise
it had often been with me.
All those occasions
I'd wished for escape
and then found it.
All those times I'd flown
without knowing
I was riding the white horse's back.

Till now, with a different view
from a different house,
a white horse
paces the field beyond my window
It seems to recognise in me
some previous complicity.
We were partners once,
we flew as one
past the rim of what we knew
and out along the edges of dreams.

Brian Moses

Storing Time

In answer to the question
'What happens to time after it is spent?'

All last year's nights
are in black bags
at Euston.

Paddington houses Lost Time
in rows of sieves
beyond Lost Property.

Bright sparkling mornings
are in clear plastic pockets
lining each horizon.

Birthdays are the grains
of gunpowder cracking fire
from Roman Candles.

Moments of supreme happiness
are held in bubbles
rising from the mouths of guppies.

Sadness lives in cinders
waiting to be streamrollered
beneath the road.

Each and every
touch and hug and kiss and smile and sneeze
is dancing with the dragonflies, up and down the breeze.

Chrissie Gittins

Jemima

Running down the garden path
Jemima, seven years old
Lifts her eyes to watch the sun
Drown in clouds of gold.
Sees her old friend smiling down
Through the chestnut tree
Her face among the branches smiles
White as ivory.
Jemima tells her secrets
Her breath is like a sigh
Wishing on a star that falls
Dying through the sky.
Jemima up the evening path
Through twilight bright as noon
Tells anyone who'll listen,
'I've been talking to the moon.'

Gareth Owen

Secret Poem

My secret is made of –
the fingertips of clouds,
the silence between heartbeats
found at a hospital bedside,
the hangman's gloves,
the stoat's bright eye,
the bullet as it slices
through the winter wind.

I found it –
on the edge of a lemon's bite,
clutched in the centre of a crocus,
held in a crisp packet,
crumpled at the side of the road
where the nettles stab
their sharp barbs
at the innocent child's hand.

This secret can –
prise open hearts made of steel,
smooth a stormy sea flat,
capture the wind,
cup the moon's shine
in an empty palm,
break apart Mount Everest
till it is powder
in a lover's pocket.

If I lost
this secret –
even the lonely mountain goat
would bleat . . .

Pie Corbett

A Minute to Midnight

**A minute to midnight
and all is still.**

For example, these are things that are still:
ornaments, coins, lamp-posts,
the cooker, Major Clark's Home for Old Folk
(just opposite our house, which is also still),
the newsagents, a hut, soap, tractors,
freshly ironed trousers draped over the chair.

**A minute to midnight
and all is still
except for the things that are moving.**

Like, for example,
rivers, clouds, leaves, flags,
creaky windmills, lungs, birds' feathers,

448

digital clocks, grass, the wind,
non-sleeping animals (especially wolves),
planet Earth, the moon, satellites in space,
toenails (well they grow, don't they),
videos that are set to record
programmes in the middle of the night,
washing lines,
mobiles above babies' cots –
and babies' eyelids, they always flicker.

John Rice

An Owl Flew in My Bedroom Once

My attic bedroom had two windows –
One that opened high above the street
And a skylight – a tile of thick glass
Like a see-through slate.
And through it fell the moonlight
Coring the darkness like an apple-peeler.
Suddenly in that long cylinder of light
Appeared the owl, mysterious and grey
In that cold moon.
He flew in silently – a piece of night adrift –
Escaped. He circled, didn't settle
On the banister or rail.
There was no rattle of his talons,
No gripe or stomp
To make him solid with their sound,
He simply floated in – turned wide – and floated out . . .
In the morning there was nothing
No down or limy dropping
Nothing to prove he'd ever been at all.

An owl flew in my bedroom once, I think.

Jan Dean

The Lost Angels

In a fish tank in France
we discovered the lost angels,
fallen from heaven and floating now
on imaginary tides.
And all along the sides of the tank,
faces peered, leered at them,
laughing, pouting,
pointing, shouting,
while hung above their heads, a sign,
Ne pas plonger les mains dans le bassin.'
Don't put your hands in the tank
– the turtles bite seriously.
And who can blame them,
these creatures with angels' wings,
drifting past like alien craft.
Who knows what signals they send
through an imitation ocean,
out of sight of sky,
out of touch with stars?

Dream on, lost angels,
then one day, one glorious day,
you'll flap your wings
and fly again.

Brian Moses

The Magic Box

I will put in the box

the swish of a silk sari on a summer night,
fire from the nostrils of a Chinese dragon,
the top of a tongue touching a tooth.

I will put in the box

a snowman with a rumbling belly,
a sip of the bluest water from Lake Lucerne,
a leaping spark from an electric fish.

I will put in the box

three violet wishes spoken in Gujarati,
the last joke of an ancient uncle
and the first smile of a baby.

I will put in the box

a fifth season and a black sun,
a cowboy on a broomstick
and a witch on a white horse.

My box is fashioned from ice and gold and steel,
with stars on the lid and secrets in the corners.
Its hinges are the toe joints
of dinosaurs.

I shall surf on my box
on the great high-rolling breaks of the wild Atlantic,
then wash ashore on a yellow beach
the colour of the sun.

Kit Wright

The Angel

Last night
I dreamed an angel came
Into our garden,

Blown off course,
From heaven to hell.

Dreamed he took shelter
And slept beneath the apple tree
At the end of the lawn,
His ragged wings wept,
A shroud over his shorn head.

When I woke this morning
I looked across the garden,
And knew that he was dead.

There he was,
Stretched out on the lawn,
Like some great swan.
His head held
Beneath broken wings.

I ran out to check his pulse.
But looking into his eyes
All that I could find
Were the lost skies
Of some distant struggle.

Paler than chalk,
His skin was too cool to touch.
I knew then
That he was dead,

So I stooped
To stroke
His fallen head,

And kissed his hair,

And as my lips
Touched his cold brow,
And as my kiss
Warmed his cold skin,

Somehow his thin body shuddered
And a glow of heat shimmered
Through his limbs.
Warm and alive,
He stretched his wings,
Now no longer ragged,

And his golden laugh
Spilled out across
Our dew-drenched lawn,
Filling that dawn
With a joy that bubbled
Through every blade of grass,
And left the clouds lit
With its own peculiar light.

I dreamed an angel late last night
But now no one believes me.
I keep a feather of bright light
Hidden beneath my bed
Just in case one of my friends
ditches disbelief.
Just in case one of my friends
grows instead
whatever it might be,
that to their cost,
those friends have sadly lost.

Pie Corbett

A Feather from an Angel

Anton's box of treasures held
a silver key and a glassy stone,
a figurine made of polished bone
and a feather from an angel.

The figurine was from Borneo,
the stone from France or Italy,
the silver key was a mystery
but the feather came from an angel.

We might have believed him if he'd said,
'The feather fell from a bleached white crow',
but he always replied, 'It's an angel's, I know,
a feather from an angel.'

We might have believed him if he'd said,
'An albatross let the feather fall',
but he had no doubt, no doubt at all,
his feather came from an angel.

'I thought I'd dreamt him one night,' he'd say,
'but in the morning I knew he'd been there;
he left a feather on my bedside chair,
a feather from an angel.'

And it seems that all my life I've looked
for the sort of belief that nothing could shift,
something simple and precious as Anton's gift,
a feather from an angel.

Brian Moses

Moon Song

Why do I eye the moon
as it shines so bright in the still night sky?

Why do I sigh and swoon
as the clouds drift softly, silently by?

Why does it pull at my heart
there through the pane in the cold blue dawn?

Why does this longing start
there in myself where the song is born?

Tony Mitton

At the End of a School Day

It is the end of a school day
　　　　and down the long drive
come bag-swinging, shouting children.
　　　　Deafened, the sky winces.
　　　　　　　The sun gapes in surprise.

Suddenly the runners skid to a stop,
　　　　stand still and stare
at a small hedgehog
　　　　curled up on the tarmac
　　　　　　　like an old, frayed cricket ball.

A girl dumps her bag, tiptoes forward
　　　　and gingerly, so gingerly
carries the creature
　　　　to the safety of a shady hedge.
　　　　　　　Then steps back, watching.

Girl, children, sky and sun
　　　　hold their breath.
There is a silence,
　　　　a moment to remember
　　　　　　　on this warm afternoon in June.

Wes Magee

Penny Piece

Sun up high,
sky so blue,
went for a walk,
nothing to do.

Branches sighing,
birds a-twitter,
down in the grass
saw something glitter.

Picked it up:
a simple penny,
nothing special,
one of many.

Kept it with me
all the same,
went on careless
till I came

upon a lake
that lay in trance,
threw my penny,
watched it dance,

spin and flicker
through the air,
down to meet
the water, where

sleeping surface
gasped awake
as that penny
hit the lake,

sending out
a circling shiver,
ripples racing,
liquid quiver,

till at last
the glassy pane
slept in silence
once again.

Lake asleep
and penny gone,
made a wish
and then walked on.

Tony Mitton

X

X-words and Wordplay

The Word Party

Loving words clutch crimson roses,
Rude words sniff and pick their noses,
Sly words come dressed up as foxes,
Short words stand on cardboard boxes,
Common words tell jokes and gabble,
Complicated words play Scrabble,
Swear words stamp around and shout,
Hard words stare each other out,
Foreign words look lost and shrug,
Careless words trip on the rug,
Long words slouch with stooping shoulders,
Code words carry secret folders,
Silly words flick rubber bands,
Hyphenated words hold hands,
Strong words show off, bending metal,
Sweet words call each other 'petal',
Small words yawn and suck their thumbs
Till at last the morning comes.
Kind words give out farewell posies . . .

Snap! The dictionary closes.

Richard Edwards

Words Behaving Badly

Words
Develop nasty habits –
Getting out of order,
Going off at tangents,
Breaking rules,
Attention seeking.
Give them fifty lines.
They take delight
In ambushing the reader,
Going round in gangs
With their unsuitable friends
Imagining they're poems!
Words –
I'd keep an eye on them
If I were you.

Sue Cowling

The Collector

Not for me woolly dolls
or football cards
pop star posters
model cars –
No, I'm into collecting adjectives . . .
    Big, fat, juicy, yummy, scrummy,
    rich and famous
    lean and keen
    kind of words.

I store them up for special occasions
    in – massive, marvellous,
        mysterious, magnificent
        adjectival boxes
    with secret seals
    and silver keys.

But, at the first stroke of the new millennium
my brother's bedside collection of !!!! marks
exploded with excitement
taking with them
the roof of our house
and
my superb adjective collection.

Request

If you should ever find an adjective
  it is probably mine.
You know the sort of word I mean
  Lonely (cloud)
  misty (lace)
  sprightly (dance)
  pretty (place)
So if you ever see one
I'm sure it will be mine
unless it isn't spelt right
  – or doesn't seem to rhyme.

Peter Dixon

What Am I?

Sometimes I rhyme,
Sometimes I don't,
Sometimes I'll tease you,
Sometimes I won't,

Some-
times
I'm
Skin-
ny,

Sometimes I take

The form

Of a square

Sometimes I ramble,
Sometimes I rap,
Sometimes I force you
To join in and clap.

Sometimes I tell you
A tale sad and long,
Sometimes I sound
Like a comical song.

Sometimes I'm shouted,
Or silently read,
Sometimes I'll drift
Like a dream, through your head.

Sometimes I'm famous
Sometimes I'm new,
But ALWAYS I'm written
For someone like YOU.

Clare Bevan

Answer?
I'm a POEM, of course!

The Haiku Monster

The haiku monster
Gobbles up the syllables
Crunching words and CHOMP!

The haiku monster
Slurps the 's' in _paghetti
Bites 'b's for _reakfast

The haiku monster
Jumbles all the telrets pu
Makes   disappear

The haiku monster
Nibbles on the v w ls nd
Chews consonants u .

The haiku monster,
Alphabet joker, plays with
The lettuce and worms.

The haiku monster
Hides rude words in the poem
And spoils bum snog vest.

Mixes up the lines
The haiku monster
Ruining all the layout.

Paul Cookson

Noisy Alphabet

Achoo! went the big sneeze,
Boom went the gong,
Click went the lock,
Ding . . . went the bell . . . Dong.
Eek! went the mouse,
Fizz went the lemonade,
Glug was the sound the boy drinking it made.
Hrumph went the camel sinking to its knees,
Inka-plinka went the cat across the piano keys.
Jingle went the harness,
Kersplat! went the pie,
La-la-la-la went the soft notes of a lullaby.
Moo went the heifer,
Neigh went the mare,
Oyez! Went the town crier standing in the square.

Plop went the raindrop,
Quack went the drake,
Roar went the tiger,
Ssss went the snake.
Too-whit went the owl,
Uh oh! meant 'Trouble's near',
Vroom went the jet,
Whoa! went the charioteer.
X-x-x went the ring pull opening the can,
Yap went the dog left behind in the van.
Z-z-z is the quietest sound in the alphabet
But with all these other noises you haven't heard it yet!

Sue Cowling

Wellingtons

I love the wild wet winter days
Of rain and slushy sleet
For it's then I fetch my Welligons
I mean my rubber Gellibongs
Oh dear I mean my Webbingtons
And pull them on my feet.

My sister Jane hates rainy days
The cold makes Mary cry
But me I've got my Wellinbots
Oh dear I mean my Bellingwots
No no I mean my Welltingots
To keep me warm and dry.

But isn't it a nuisance
Isn't it a shame
That though I love you Wellibongs
I just can't say your name.

Gareth Owen

A Bad Case of Fish

A chip-shop owner's in the dock
on a charge of assault and battery.
The monkfish takes the oath:
So help me Cod . . .

The courtroom's packed with lost soles.
The crabby judge can't find his plaice
or read the prosecution's whiting.
And what sort of fish is a saveloy, anyway?

The young skates are getting bored.
They start skateboarding down the aisles.
The scampi scamper to and fro.
The eels are dancing congers.

But the case is cut and dried.
It's all wrapped up. (Just look
in the evening paper.) Next,
the Krayfish twins . . .

Philip Gross

Size-Wise

Our teacher Mr Little's really tall.
He's twice the size of our helper Mrs Small.
'Were you big when you were little?'
Sandra asked him.
'I was Little when I was little,
but I've always been big!'
he said with a grin.
'Have you always been small?'
Sandra asked Mrs Small.
'No,' said Mrs Small.
'I was Short before I got married,
then I became Small.
But,' she added, 'I've always been little.'
'That's the long and the short of it,'
said Mr Little.
'I've always been big and Little,
but she used to be little and Short,
and now she's little and Small.'

John Foster

If I Were the Leader

If I were the duke
Of oh-what-a-fluke
Then life would be a ball.

If I were the head
Of lying-in-bed
I'd never get up at all.

If I were in charge
Of everyone large
I wouldn't be pushed about.

If I were the boss
Of ever-so-cross
I'd stamp and scream and shout.

If I were the prince
Of only-a-rinse
There'd be no showers or baths.

If I were the lord
Of never-be-bored
We'd have no rain or maths.

If I were the chief
Of bacon-and-beef
I'd eat whatever I chose.

If I were the king
Of everything
I'd really get up your nose.

Nick Toczek

Tenpin Bowling

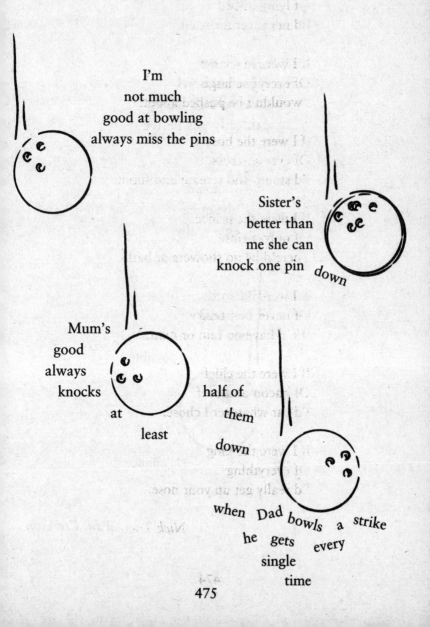

I'm
not much
good at bowling
always miss the pins

Sister's
better than
me she can
knock one pin down

Mum's
good
always
knocks   half of
at   them
least
                        down

when Dad bowls a strike
he   gets   every
single
time

2nd bowl

my
first bowl
was rubbish things
can only get better

should
be quite
easy really

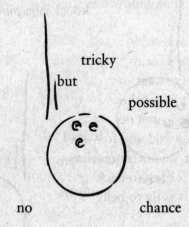

tricky

but

possible

no   chance

Paul Cookson

An Army Marches on its Stomach?

We don't march on our stomachs
Prefer to use our feet
They're nippier over bracken
And miles of soggy peat

Lindsay MacRae

Poetry Jump-up

Tell me if Ah seeing right
Take a look down de street

Words dancin
words dancin
till dey sweat
words like fishes
jumpin out a net
words wild and free
joinin de poetry revelry
words back to back
words belly to belly

Come on everybody
come and join de poetry band
dis is poetry carnival
dis is poetry bacchanal
when inspiration call
take yu pen in yu hand
if yu don't have a pen
take yu pencil in yu hand
if yu don't have a pencil
what the hell
so long as de feeling start to swell
just shout de poem out

Words jumpin off de page
tell me if Ah seein right
words like birds
jumpin out a cage
take a look down de street
words shakin dey waist
words shaking dey bum
words wit black skin
words wit white skin
words wit brown skin
words wit no skin at all
words huggin up words
an sayin I want to be a poem today
rhyme or no rhyme
I is a poem today
I mean to have a good time

Words feelin hot hot hot
big words feelin hot hot hot
lil words feelin hot hot hot
even sad words can't help
tappin dey toe
to de riddum of de poetry band

Dis is poetry carnival
dis is poetry bacchanal
so come on everybody
join de celebration
all yu need is plenty perspiration
an a little inspiration
plenty perspiration
an a little inspiration

John Agard

Y

Young and Old

Grandpa's Soup

No one makes soup like my Grandpa's,
with its diced carrots the perfect size
and its diced potatoes the perfect size
and its wee soft bits –
what are their names?
and its big bit of hough,
which rhymes with loch, floating
like a rich island in the middle of the soup sea.

I say, Grandpa, Grandpa, your soup is the best soup in the
    whole world.
And Grandpa says, Och,
which rhymes with hough and loch.
Och, don't be daft,
because he's shy about his soup, my Grandpa.
He knows I will grow up and pine for it.
I will get ill and desperately need it.
I will long for it my whole life after he is gone.
Every soup will become sad and wrong after he is gone.

He knows when I'm older I will avoid soup altogether.
Oh Grandpa, Grandpa, why is your soup so glorious? I say
tucking into my fourth bowl in a day.

Barley! That's the name of the wee soft bits. Barley.

Jackie Kay

Visiting Grandad in the Home

His life is a half-circle
Of chairs by the TV.
His eyes come alive
And he waves at me,

But he calls me Simon,
And that's my dad's name,
And we talk about the weather
And the England game.

Then his face seems to slip,
His smile fades away
As he falls over backwards
Into yesterday.

And he talks to Grandma
Even though she isn't there,
And he's telling stories
To an empty chair.

And it's time for me to go
And he doesn't see me leave
And he won't know that I've been
But I really do believe

That the minutes I sit there
Mean an awful lot
Whether Grandad can remember them

Or not.

Ian McMillan

When Granny

Song-bird shut dem mout' an lissen,
Church bell don' bother to ring,
All de little stream keep quiet
When mi Granny sing.

De sun up in de sky get jealous,
Him wish him got her style,
For de whole place full o' brightness
When mi Granny smile.

First a happy soun' jus' bubblin'
From her belly, low an' sof',
Den a thunderclap o' merriment
When mi Granny laugh.

De tree branch dem all start swingin',
Puss an' dawg begin to prance,
Everyt'ing ketch de happy fever
When mi Granny dance.

All o' we look out fe Granny
Mek sure dat she satisfy,
For de whole worl' full o' sadness
When mi Granny cry.

Valerie Bloom

Grannie

I stayed with her when I was six then went
To live elsewhere when I was eight years old.
For ages I remembered her faint scent
Of lavender, the way she'd never scold
No matter what I'd done, and most of all
The way her smile seemed, somehow, to enfold
My whole world like a warm, protective shawl.

I knew that I was safe when she was near,
She was so tall, so wide, so large, she would
Stand mountainous between me and my fear,
Yet oh, so gentle, and she understood
Every hope and dream I ever had.
She praised me lavishly when I was good,
But never punished me when I was bad.

Years later war broke out and I became
A soldier and was wounded while in France.
Back home in hospital, still very lame,
I realized suddenly that circumstance
Had brought me close to that small town where she
Was living still. And so I seized the chance
To write and ask if she could visit me.

She came. And I still vividly recall
The shock that I received when she appeared
That dark cold day. Huge grannie was so small!
A tiny, frail, old lady. It was weird.
She hobbled through the ward to where I lay
And drew quite close and, hesitating, peered.
And then she smiled: and love lit up the day.

Vernon Scannell

Grandma

Grandma was always there
Always had silver hair
Lived next door

But when we visited her
In the nursing home
Part of her was missing

Who are you? she asked me.
I told her

Remember how we used to
Go to the market
To buy scraps of silk?
She smiled.

Remember you took me to
The Seaside Bingo
And I won a dartboard?
She nodded.

Remember me and Grandad
Playing football on the yard
And breaking the shed door?
We both laughed.

And when the bell rang
And the nurse said
It's time to go
I held Grandma's hand
And she said,
Who are you?

Roger Stevens

Grandma's Jigsaw Puzzle

Grandma wanted to find the house
where she lived as a child
at the beginning of time
when grass was greener
when light was brighter
when sound was sharper
and a pound
was worth twenty shillings

Dad took us round factories
and schools and new houses
where there were once fields
and footpaths and allotments.
We gazed at signs and brick walls
trying to piece together clues
And grandma said, It was so long ago.
She said, It was so long ago

And in the end,
the jigsaw puzzle in grandma's head
was just too difficult to solve

Roger Stevens

Grandmother

Rain falls on warm tin roofs
    like a thousand pearls.

The air is thick with ripe mangoes,
    chickens scratch in the yard,

  Bibi stands on the veranda
  holding me in a tight hug,
  her perfume of betel nut.

  On the night she died
  I dreamt of her:
  of carrying water
  to quench her thirst.

Contributor to First Words

The Long Grass

I lost my favourite football
in the long grass
thirty years ago.
We searched for hours,
for days, for weeks on end.
But could we find it? No.
The air will have escaped by now.

The fountain pen
my brother gave me
disappeared back then,
left for a moment;
but I can't remember
where or when.
Who waved a magic wand?

Somewhere between the front door
and eternity
I lost a bunch of keys.
Climbed on chairs to search for them.
Searched on hands and knees.
I asked my friends.
They have no news.

The wallet
given as a Christmas present?
Gone.
Gone with all its money
and the scraps of paper I had written on.
Will someone ever
hand it in?

I misplace people's names.
Their faces I remember, yes,
but who they are
and when we met
I cannot even guess.
My memory is decomposing
in the grass.

My toys have gone.
The diary I kept
when I was seventeen:
its list of favourite films,
the dreams of who I might have been.
Could they have wound up
in the bin?

With one brief chapter
left to read
I left my book
somewhere sensible.
I've no idea where.
Will you help me look?
I can tell you what each character is like.

I miss my father, too.
I'd like to find him
but I don't know how.
Perhaps he's wading
through the long grass even now,
calling our names;
trying to get home.

Stephen Knight

Sardines

You slip behind your parents' clothes
   in nineteen sixty-eight,
pull shut the wardrobe door, then
   curl into a ball.
                    You wait.

It's very still in there. So quiet.
    Your chin rests on your knees.
A long fur-coat is tickling
    so much you want to sneeze.

A year goes by. Neil Armstrong walks
    the surface of the moon
as slow as honey, while you think
    'Someone will find me soon!'

You fiddle with your father's ties.
    The earth crawls round the sun
and footsteps pass the wardrobe door.
    – It could be anyone!

The world outside turns decimal
    and all the old coins go
the way of dinosaurs, of early
    morning mist, of snow.

It's very quiet in there. So still.
    Your knees support your chin
while you whisper, 'Any minute now
    someone will burst in . . .'

Fashions change: hemlines fall and rise.
    Hands sometimes reach inside
to take a shirt or dress away –
    the door is opened wide

and then it's closed, and then it's dark
   once more. Leaves grow. Leaves fall.
The earth crawls round the sun again.
   (You almost *hear* it crawl.)

One day in nineteen eighty-five
   you think about your life
alone; but there's room for neither
   children nor a wife

in there. It's very still. So quiet.
   Your chin rests on your knees.
Sometimes you whistle in that dark
   like wind through broken trees.

'No one's going to find,' you say,
   'my perfect hiding-place.
Not now.' It's nineteen ninety-nine.
   The planet spins through space,

the trees grow fat with overcoats
   and you, you droop until
(at last) you fall asleep.
                    Good night.
It's quiet in there, and still.
So still.
            So very still.

Stephen Knight

Red Running Shoes

I wore some other girl's red running shoes
with real spikes like rose thorns under my foot.

I got into position: my limbs seriously tense,
one knee on the asphalt, one foot flat, all that.

I crouched over, hands down, like a predator
ready for prey; and took off, took flight

on the red running track, so fast I could be fear
running, a live fright, a chance vision.

My dark hair wild in the wind.
My arms pounding light years, thin air, euphoria.

I flew past in some other girl's red running shoes
round the red track, near the railway line.

I raced straight towards the future.
The past was left standing behind, waving.

I ran and ran; my feet became the land.
I couldn't tell if the ground was moving under my feet

shifting sand, or if I might ever just stop like a heartbeat.
It felt as if I could run for ever, hard pounding feet

until I ran into myself, years on
sat still, heavy, pasty forty, groaning, the streak lightning
   gone.

Jackie Kay

Righting Wrongs

Stamping on ants
was something I did
as a kid.
Earwigs too
from holes in our fences.
I stick-twisted terror
into tiny lives.
I trapped flies in jars
then fed spiders.
A colossal creature
grew rounder and fatter
on sacrifices
from me.

These days I'm making up
for the slaughter,
setting life against life,
airlifting bees from
the paddling pool,
shifting snails away from feet
and swooping down
to remove lost worms
from the frizzling heat
of the sun.

And O Great Protector
of ants, flies, wasps, mozzies, slugs
and all other such irritants –
I hope somehow that with these deeds
I can erase a little
from the list of my past mistakes,
from the tally of tiny creatures
I eagerly destroyed as a boy.

Brian Moses

Z

Zapping Aliens

WOrmhOles in Space

Intergalactic, Outerspace EarthwOrms,
flying the cOsmOs:
                         fantastic!

FrOm red stars tO white stars,
frOm planets tO mOOns
they zap,
                   with the snap! Of elastic

Intergalactic, Outerspace EarthwOrms,
but aren't they a little absurd?

NO,
they just need tO escape

– thrOugh wOrmhOles in space –
frOm thOse ravenOus early birds.

Mike Johnson

My Stepdad Is an Alien

I'd suspected for some time.
I finally got up the courage
to talk to him about it.

I think you're an alien, I told him.

Nonsense, he said. Why do you think that?

You're bald. You don't have any hair
anywhere.

That's not that unusual, he said.

Well, you've got one green eye
and one blue one.

That doesn't make me an alien, he replied.

You can make the toaster work
without turning it on.

That's just a trick, he smiled.

Sometimes I hear you
talking to Mum in a weird alien language.

I'm learning Greek
and Mum lets me practise on her.

What about your bright blue tail?

Ah, he said thoughtfully.
You're right, of course.
So, the tail gave it away, did it?

Roger Stevens

My Rocket Ship

T
Od
Ay I
Made
A rocket ship
That can fly
Me to the stars.
It's made from
Plastic bottles
Cardboard boxes
And jam jars.
Its engine is a
Broken
Clock,
That was left under the stairs.
The seats are made from socks and shirts
That no one   ever wears.

Ian Bland

The Amazing Adventures
of SPACE BOY

Featuring COSMIC CAT

Every space mission
would take an age of preparation

Every Saturday
on returning from the Mega Store

Watched and guided
by the silent Cosmic Cat
Space Boy would begin . . .

First he would assemble
a monitor screen
(a cardboard box
with a picture of the moon
scribbled on in wax crayon)

Next Space Boy would
clamp on his plutonium space watch
(tin foil wrapped around his wrist)

Then Space Boy would adjust his space visor
(more tin foil)

From here Space Boy would prepare
a space suit for Cosmic Cat
(more tin foil)
which Cosmic Cat would refuse to wear
on account of the fact that
she had radar whiskers
crypto-fur and a tail-antenna

Next Space Boy would
tune in to the soundwaves of the cosmos
for news of alien sightings or invasions
(listen to the radio)

Then Space Boy inspects
the universe through his bio-force binary binoculars
(two toilet rolls covered with glued-on Cheerios AND tin
    foil)

Finally Space Boy would ensure
that he was free from chronic-cosmic-contamination
(have a quick bath)

And a billion light years later
as Space Boy and Cosmic Cat
are whirling their way
through the intergalactic chaos of
encountering aliens
battling through black holes
and avoiding catastrophic galactic storms –
a horrible other-worldly screech
would reach their end of the universe
and stop them dead in their tracks:

'JAMES! Aren't you in bed yet?'

James Carter

Aliens Stole My Underpants

To understand the ways
of alien beings is hard,
and I've never worked it out
why they landed in my backyard.

And I've always wondered why
on their journey from the stars,
these aliens stole my underpants
and took them back to Mars.

They came on a Monday night
when the weekend wash had been done,
pegged out on the line
to be dried by the morning sun.

Mrs Driver from next door
was a witness at the scene
when aliens snatched my underpants –
I'm glad that they were clean!

It seems they were quite choosy
as nothing else was taken.
Do aliens wear underpants
or were they just mistaken?

I think I have a theory
as to what they wanted them for,
they needed to block off a draught
blowing in through the spacecraft door.

Or maybe some Mars museum
wanted items brought back from Space.
Just think, my pair of Y-fronts
displayed in their own glass case.

And on the label beneath
would be written where they got 'em
and how such funny underwear
once covered an Earthling's bottom!

Brian Moses

In Love with an Alien

Sue fell in love with an alien
And what was wrong with that?
She liked his many winking eyes
and the antennae under his hat.

She liked the way he sang to her
In that whispering windswept voice.
She liked the way he listened to her
Unlike most of the boys.

She liked his way of knowing
Who was outside the door
And she liked the way his many feet
Danced on the disco floor.

Sue fell in love with an alien;
He said that he would write . . .
Now she sits alone in her bedroom,
Staring into the starry night.

Trevor Millum

Football, As Understood by a Martian

Simple!
Kick round object
over long muddy field.
Try to aim it between two sticks –
for kicks!

Judith Nicholls

Cat Message

Shemu the cat
Whose ancestors
Prowled amongst the pyramids
Today received a special visitor

Neferhotep
Ambassador
From the constellation of Orion

Upon Neferhotep's
Departure
Shemu tried her best
To warn her mistress
Of Neferhotep's message

The Earth is about to be invaded

Shemu lay on the carpet
And made letter shapes
With her body
I – N – V –A – S – I – O – N

Shemu brought twigs and scraps of bark
Into the kitchen
Arranged in the symbol O-ki-hran
Which is Orionese for
You are about to be invaded by hideous aliens
From the constellation Andromeda

Shemu even reprogrammed the video
To play Star Trek tapes

But Shemu's only reward
For her efforts
Was some tinned cat-food

Humans, thought Shemu,
Can be so . . .
Dumb.

Roger Stevens

The Snake's Revenge

You could never imagine me,
not in a zillion years,
I'm far beyond the scope of
your wildest nightmares or fears.

But I'm here, at the edge of your universe,
a creature of immeasurable girth.
Hatred has made me huge, and now
I'm the snake that will swallow the earth.

And I'm moving ever closer,
I've already gobbled up stars,
I've unhinged my jaws and soon I'll be ready
to take a crack at Mars.

And when I finally reach you
I'll tell you now what I'll do
I shall wrap my coils round your planet
and squeeze the breath out of you.

And this will be my revenge
from the time that I was cursed,
for eternity spent on my belly,
for the dust that I ate, for my thirst.

And remember well, if you will,
for a snake is nobody's friend,
I was there at the very beginning
and I'll be there at the end.

For the world won't finish in flame
or by drowning in a flood.
It won't be wholly engulfed
in an ocean of angry mud.

There'll be no explosion, no fracture,
no tremors from a last earthquake.
I tell you now, this world will end
in the belly of a snake.

Brian Moses

Song in Space

When man first flew beyond the sky
He looked back into the world's blue eye.
Man said: What makes your eye so blue?
Earth said: The tears in the oceans do.
Why are the seas so full of tears?
Because I've wept so many thousand years.
Why do you weep as you dance through space?
Because I am the mother of the human race.

Adrian Mitchell

Star Gazing

At midnight through my window
I spy with wondering eye
The far-off stars and planets
Sprinkled on the sky.

There the constant North Star
Hangs above our trees
And there the Plough and Sirius
And the distant Pleiades.

Star on star counting
Each one a raging sun
And the sky one endless suburb
With all her lights left on.

How strange it is that certain stars
Whose distant lights still glow
Vanished in that sea of space
Three million years ago.

And if I stare too long a time
The stars swim in my eyes
Drifting towards my bedroom
Down the vast slope of the skies.

And, mesmerized, I wonder,
Will *our* Earth someday die?
Spreading her fabric and her dreams
In fragments on the sky.

And then my imagination
Sees in some distant dawn
A young girl staring skywards
On a planet still unborn.

And will she also wonder,
Was there ever life out there?
Before the whole thing vanished
Like a dream into the air.

Gareth Owen

Glossary of Terms

Not sure what we mean by Haiku? Forgotten what a verb is? Here is an explanation of the words used in and relevant to this book.

Acrostic
This is a poetic form that uses the initial letters of a key word at the beginning of each line, e.g.

Creeps through the darkness,
Along the garden wall,
Tail swaying.

You can also hide the key word within the poem, e.g.

Animal Riddle

> Like a small Bear
> > bundles over the dark road,
> > brushes pAst the front gate,
> > as if she owns the joint.
> > rolls the Dustbin,
> > like an expert barrel rider,
> tucks into yesterday's Garbage,
> > crunches worms for titbits.
> wakes us from dEep sleep,
> > blinks back at torchlight.
> our midnight feasteR,
> > ghost-friend,
> > moon-lit,
> > zebra bear.

Pie Corbett

Action Verse
These are rhymes that involve an action. They are usually performed for small children!

Adjective
A word or phrase that is added or linked to a noun to describe it.
e.g. the *red* dress.

Glossary of Terms

Adverb

A word or phrase which describes a verb. Many end in 'ly'.
e.g. she ran *quickly*.

Alliteration

This is when poets use the same sound close by.
e.g. *the cruel cat cautiously crept by*.
Alliteration is very useful because it draws the reader's attention to the words. It makes the words memorable – often advertisers use alliteration for this reason (Buy a *Ticktock* today). You can have great fun with alliterative sentences by creating Tongue-Twisters. You may know this one:
Red lorry, yellow lorry.

Alphabet Poem

This is a poem written using the letters of the alphabet, e.g.

A is an ant,
B is a baboon . . .

Assonance

This is the repetition of vowel sounds close to each other, creating echoes.
e.g. *the figure gave a low groan*.

Ballad

This is a formal poem or song that is meant to be performed aloud. Ballads tell stories, using a regular pattern, usually with verses and a chorus, e.g.

'O Mary, go and call the cattle home,
    And call the cattle home,
    And call the cattle home,
    Across the sands of Dee!'
The western wind was wild and dank with foam,
    And all alone went she.

From 'The Sands of Dee' by Charles Kingsley.

Blank Verse

This is poetry that is written with a rhythm and metre but has no rhymes. Shakespeare often wrote in blank verse.

Glossary of Terms

Calligram

This is a picture poem made of letters representing an aspect of the poem. For instance, if the word chosen was 'shake' the writer might write the word using a wobbly typeface, '*s h a k e*'. In the example below the words are leaning across to reflect the meaning.
The sloping wall.

Chant

This is a rhyme that has a strong beat and rhythm. It can be chanted aloud to good effect.

Characterization

The process by which a poet or writer creates an impression of a character.
e.g. overuse of negative words and events could create the character of a failure.

Things *haven't* been too good just lately
Speeding bullets *overtake* me
My dizzy spells and *fear* of heights
Inconvenience all my flights

From 'A Superhero Sends a Letter Home' by Paul Cookson.

Choral Poem

A poem for speaking aloud by a whole group.

Cinquain

This was invented by the American poet Adelaide Crapsey – it is rather like a haiku – consisting of five lines, using twenty-two syllables, arranged in a sequence 2, 4, 6, 8, 2. The last line is often a surprise.

Classic Poem

This is a poem that has stood the test of time. Its author may be dead but the poem is considered to be sufficiently memorable still to be printed and read.

Clerihew

This is a four-line comic verse, with two rhyming couplets (AABB). The first line is the name of the person being written about. It was invented by Edmund Clerihew Bentley. Children would be unlikely to come across this form.

Cliché

This is an overused, stale phrase or word combination.
e.g. the cotton-wool clouds.

Glossary of Terms

Collage Poem

This is a list poem, where each line adds a new image. Many writers use this technique, e.g.

I remember the waves rushing up the beach.
I remember the gulls dipping over the headland.
I remember the black, jagged rocks . . .

Concrete Poem

This is a sort of shape poem where the design of the words adds extra meaning to the poem; it relies on the layout of the words for full impact. The Scottish poet Ian Hamilton Finlay literally made poems out of stone and put them in his garden!

Consonance

This is the repetition of consonants that are close to each other, to create echoes. e.g. the quick click of his heels . . .

Conversation

This is a poem written as if there was a conversation taking place. Often good for performing aloud!

Counting Rhyme

Rhymes that use numbers,
e.g. One, two, buckle my shoe . . .

Couplet

Two consecutive, paired lines of poetry, e.g.

Nor I half turn to go yet turning stay,
Remember me when no more day by day

Determiner

A word that tells you more about a noun, e.g.

A dog
Each dog
Every dog
The dog

Glossary of Terms

Dialogue
A conversation between two parties. May be spoken or written.

Elegy
This is a poem or song which is written/performed for a person (or an animal) that has died.

Epitaph
You find epitaphs engraved on tombstones, often in brief poetic form. They sometimes recall aspects of the deceased!

Eye (or Sight) Rhyme
These are words that look as if they might rhyme but do not.
e.g. cough/through.

Figurative Language
Use of metaphor or simile to create an impression or mood. Figurative language helps to build up a picture in the reader's mind. Poets use it all the time!

Free Verse
Poetry not constrained by metrical or rhyming patterns. (Some would say that sometimes free verse is just an excuse for not working hard at creating a form!)

Future Tense
A way of writing about things that will happen in the future.
e.g. tomorrow I *will go* to the shops.

Haiku
This is a very popular Japanese form of poetry. It is brief, related to the seasons/nature, expresses a sense of awe or insight, written using concrete sense images and not abstractions, in the present tense. It is often written as three lines, of seventeen syllables arranged in a sequence 5, 7, 5, though not necessarily. A verbal snapshot, capturing the essence of a moment/scene. Some haiku are only a line or two. The idea is to capture a moment, e.g.

Flies stalk the cup's rim
Washing their hands, fidgeting
In the sullen heat.

Glossary of Terms

Half-rhyme
These are words which almost rhyme.
e.g. grip/grab.

Homonym
A word with the same spelling as another, but a different meaning.
e.g. the *calf* was eating/my *calf* was aching.

Pronunciation may be different.
e.g. a *lead* pencil/the dog's *lead*.

Idiom
A phrase often used that is not meant literally. Its meaning is understood by the people who use it, but cannot be inferred from knowledge of the individual words.
e.g. over the moon, under the weather, thick as two short planks.

Imagery
This is when you are using language to create a vivid sensory image or picture in the reader's mind. This is done with similes and metaphors but also by carefully selecting the right word.

Internal Rhyme
This is when the poet puts rhymes within lines, e.g.

Lizard cars cruise by.
Their radiators *grin*.
Thin headlights stare . . .

Kenning
This is a sort of riddle. It was used in Old English and Norse poetry to name something without using its name, e.g. mouse catcher (cat). The Anglo Saxons named their swords in this way, e.g. bone cruncher.

Limerick
This is a popular form of funny poetry that is actually not easy to write! You need a pattern consisting of five lines. These lines follow a thirty-six-syllable count in a sequence of 8, 8, 6, 6, 8 with rhyme scheme AABBA.

List Poem
This is a poem that is written rather like a list, using the same repeating phrase to introduce each idea, e.g.

I saw a fish on fire.
I saw a bird swim in oil.
I saw . . .

Metaphor
Metaphors are rather like similes, except in a simile you say that one thing is like another. In a metaphor you just say that one thing IS another – so you are writing about something as if it was something else. 'The moon is like a smile' is a simile. 'The moon is a smile' is a metaphor.

Metre
This is the term used to describe the organization of poetry by the pattern of regular rhythm.

Monologue
This is when a character speaks aloud. Monologues are found in plays but some poems are written to be spoken aloud by a character.

Narrative Poem
This is quite simply a story poem. Ballads are a form of narrative poem.

Nonsense Poem
This is poetry that uses nonsense words ('Twas Brillig and the slithy toves) or writes about nonsensical events (We put on our pigeons and swam through the custard).

Noun
A noun is the name of a thing, person, place or idea.

Nursery Rhyme
This is a rhyme that parents sing to very small children.

Onomatopoeia
These are words that sound like their meaning.
e.g. the busy bee buzzes.

Oral Poem
This is a poem that has been passed down through the generations by word of mouth.

Past Tense
A way of writing about things that happened in the past.
e.g. I *went to* the shops.

Performance Poem
This is a poem intended for performance. Often direct and lively, using rhythm and rhyme. Great fun to join in with. Of course, most poems can be performed!

Personification
This is a form of metaphor and great fun to write. It is when you take an object and pretend it has come alive – rather like sprinkling Disney dust on to broomsticks so that they get up and start dancing, e.g

The wind moaned.
The trees stooped down.
The bushes whispered.

Playground Chant/Rhyme
This is a rhyme that children tell in the playground. It is often used for skipping, clapping, ball-bouncing games, ring games and dipping.

Powerful Verb
A powerful verb draws the attention of the reader to the action. It brings energy to the writing by being more extreme and descriptive, e.g.

'Get out!' she *said* loudly.
'Get out!' she *screamed*.

Prayer
Words spoken to a god.

Present Tense
A way of writing that expresses actions or states at the time of speaking.
e.g. I am *going to* the shops.

Pun
This is a play on words, where a word has two meanings.
e.g. the book is not red/the book is not read.

Rap
This is a lively form of poetry that uses strong rhythm and rapid pace. It is often

performed with music and is rather like rapid, rhyming speech.

Refrain
This is a repeated chorus.

Renga
These are a series of haiku that are linked together. Each haiku picks up on a link from the previous one. Sometimes written by different poets to form a series.

Rhyme
These are words that make the same end sounds, e.g. dig/fig. Half-rhymes are words that almost rhyme, e.g. slip/sleep. End rhymes fall at the end of the lines in poetry. Internal rhymes come in the middle of the lines. Eye rhymes look as if they should rhyme but do not, e.g. cough/through.

Rhythm
Poems should have rhythm so that the poem is memorable. Rhythm is the more or less regular alternation of light and heavy beats in speech or music to provide a beat.

Riddle
A form of poetry where the subject is hidden and the reader has to guess what is being written about.

Shape Poem
This is a poem that is written in a shape. The shape usually reflects the subject of the poem.

Simile
Similes are used a lot by poets. A simile is when you are saying that one thing is like another, to create a picture in the reader's mind. There are two sorts of simile:
1. Using like, e.g. a saddle *like* a mushroom.
2. Using as, e.g. as slow *as* grass growing.

Song
Words that are intended to be accompanied by music. They often have several verses with a repeated chorus in between.

Sonnet
This is a special form of poetry. It was popular with Italian poets, and began in the thirteenth century. It is a poem of fourteen lines, often following a rhyme scheme.

Glossary of Terms

Style
The style is the way in which the writer expresses what they want to say.
e.g. Edward Lear is known for his nonsense verse while Shakespeare is famous for blank verse and iambic pentameter (ten beats per line with stresses on alternate syllables starting with the second).

Surrealism
This is a form of writing that is rather crazy and dream-like – where all sorts of impossible things happen.

Syllabic Poem
Syllabic verse is organized by the pattern of syllables per line.

Syllable
Each beat in a word is a syllable.
e.g. *cat* has one syllable but *kitten* has two (kit-ten).

Synonym
Words which have the same, or very similar, meaning, e.g. wet/damp. Avoids overuse of any word; adds variety.

Tanka
This is a Japanese form based on haiku with two additional lines. Traditionally, when a member of the Japanese court wrote a haiku, the receiver would add two extra lines and return it. It uses a pattern of 5, 7, 5, 7, 7 syllables.

Thin Poem
A shape poem written down or across the page with only a few letters or words per line so that it is thin!

Tone
The way in which something within a piece of writing is said so that it reveals the attitudes and presuppositions of the author. Whether the writer uses sarcasm or humour, etc., to put across their opinion will change what it means to the reader.

Tongue-twister
These are short lines which alliterate or rhyme. They are often very hard to say, especially when repeated quickly, e.g. unique, New York.

Glossary of Terms

Traditional Rhyme
This is a rhyme that has been known for many years. Many of them are nursery rhymes.

Verb
A word or group of words which names an action or state of being. A Doing Word.

Word Puzzle
A range of word games, often in poetic form.

Index of Poem Types

Index of Poem Types

Index of Poem Types

Index of Poem Types

Index of Poem Types

Index of Poem Types

Index of Poem Types

Index of Poem Types

Index of Poem Types

Index of Poem Types

Index of Poem Types

Index of Poem Types

A–Z of Advice for Young Poets

Audience – present poems by performing, making posters, post-its, use email or stick them in a bottle and let them float away.

Brainstorm – look or think about your subject – write quickly. Cherry pick the best ideas. Train the brain to be quick – and remember – the first thought is not always the best!

Concentrate – learn to look carefully. When writing, blot everything else out. Write furiously.

Decide – writing is about choosing words and ideas. Read your work aloud to see and hear how it sounds. Listen to your own writing as if you had never heard it before.

Experiment – try out different words and combinations. Be brave and try for new combinations – use 'cockerel lava' rather than 'red lava'.

Feelings – write about what moves you. It must matter.

Grow – let poems have time to grow. Come back to them after a while and see how they sound!

Habit – keep on practising; write every day. Don't worry about 'getting it right' – 'get it written', then go back over it!

Imagine – take what you know and invent a bit; play 'what if . . .' or 'supposing'. Cars could break-dance and telegraph poles pick teeth.

Juggle – keep throwing the words up into the air, testing them out.

Know – write about what you know about – interests and obsessions.

Look – become a close observer of the world.

Mimic – notice how other writers gain their effects – use their patterns for practice. Read daily and learn good poems – let beautiful language live forever in your mind.

Notebook – keep a notebook to jot down observations, ideas, and words, things people say, funny things, rhythms and . . . wrestle with words.

Opposites – try words and ideas that conflict – 'loud silences' and 'soft granite'.

Play – play with ideas, so that in the window you see a tulip blossom, so that the moon grins and the sun is a giant gobstopper.

Question – interrogate the world, make the world speak. Ask tigers who made them and why the stars are so silent. Then reply.

Recreate – use words to preserve your experience – to recreate the world. To explain yourself to the world and the world to yourself.

Secrets – use your imagination to discover the secret world – of stones and snakes . . .

Trim – avoid using too many words or they'll cancel each other out.

Unique – find your own ideas and fresh combinations.

Voice/s – try writing as if you were a creature, an object or someone else, write in role – and give the world a voice.

Word hoard – get in the habit of collecting and tasting the flavour of words.

X-ray – look so hard that you can see to the heart.

Yourself – put yourself into your poems as well as the subject.

Zeal – write with energy, enjoyment and celebration.

A–Z of Poetry-reading Ideas

Assembly – hold a poetry assembly where each class performs poems.

Buy words – which words would you buy or borrow from a poem? Keep a notebook to store tasty words.

Cut up and close reading – cut up a poem for someone else to reassemble – by word, line or verse. Or, cut out words and leave spaces to be filled.

Drawing – illustrate a poem – create poem posters.

Enthusiasm – discuss what you liked in a poem, what you didn't like – draw up a desert island list of top ten poems or poets. Hold a vote across the school.

Feelings – read and discuss what poems make you feel and think. Write down or share your first impressions.

Gossip – chat about poets and poems. Hold regular 'recommendation' sessions where you promote a poet or poem that you think others will enjoy.

Highlights – which are the highlights of a poem? Which is a poet's best poem and why? Use a highlighter to identify key words or lines.

Imitate – imitage poetic ideas or patterns and write a poem yourself.

Journals – keep a poetry journal – each week stick in a new poem that you like.

Know it by heart – learn poems by heart. Chant, perform and sing poems out loud.

Letters – write to poets . . . or to characters in their poems.

Memories – what memories does a poem stir – what do you see in your mind, what does it remind you of?

Newspaper headlines – create a newspaper headline and article about a poem or what is happening in a poem, especially narrative poetry.

Organize – a poetry reading or poetry day. Invite poets into school for book weeks or arts festivals.

Performance – perform poems – make tapes and videos. Send these to other classes or schools.

Question – ask questions about poems – what puzzles you? What are you not certain about? Discuss mysteries. Remember – not everything makes sensible sense – sometimes poems have to be experienced and not just understood.

Reread – keep rereading a poem to let its meaning creep up on you – and to let the words sink forever into your mind.

Swap – swap poems over. Find one you think your partner would enjoy.

Title – hide the title of a poem – what might the poem be called?

Underline – use a coloured pencil to underline, star or circle parts of a poem that are of interest – likes, dislikes, puzzles or patterns.

Video – video a reading or class performance of a poem. Put on a poetry show.

Weekly – have a poet of the week or month – read their poems each day.

X-ray – put on your X-ray vision when reading – try to see and listen to the heart of a poem.

Yardstick – collect a few poems that act as your poetic yardstick – what is a really good poem by which all others have to be judged – which are the great ones . . . And why?

Zodiac – create a zodiac of poems – one for each star (or month) sign.

A–Z of Poetry Activities

This alphabet contains a couple of ideas for each section of the anthology.

A – The Ark and Other Creatures – write and illustrate a 'Beware' poster for Barry's Budgie. Swap over animal sounds, e.g. gerbils roar, cats bark, dogs hoot, cows squeak . . .

B – Boys' Stuff – make a list of possible new Olympic Sports that you might do well at, e.g. watching *EastEnders*, cracking knuckles, eating Shredded Wheat . . . List ingredients for a boy, e.g. puppy dog's tails, scruffy trainers, cold spaghetti . . .

C – Celebrations and Festivals – make a class time-line of celebrations and festivals, including all the birthdays, important days for different members of the class. Hot seat one of Herod's henchmen.

D – Dinosaurs, Dragons and Dodos – make a list of animals that got left off the ark, e.g. unicorns. Invent instructions that would help you see a dragon.

E – Elements, Seasons and the Natural World – illustrate a poem, e.g. Icy Fingers. Choose a favourite time of year and list what you like, e.g. I love the sun warming the roof tiles. I love the swallows scribbling on the sky . . .

F – Friends and Families – role play the conversation between Megan and Kelly. Write your own fantasy Christmas or Birthday wish list.

G – Girls' Stuff – add to Clare Bevan's list of things that mermaids learn at school – what do fairies or ogres learn? Find a box and collect your own treasure trove of objects – write a list of memories and wishes to keep in the box.

H – Home Life – write a letter to Mum or Dad, or another adult, giving excuses for something that you have done wrong (excuses for late homework – an alien stole it!). Write a list of the special music you can hear in your school or home.

I – Impossible, Incredible – list what the kleptomaniac might steal – clouds from the sky, green from the grass . . . draw a picture that has had parts of it stolen!

J – Journeys – draw a cartoon version of 'The Cruise of the Bumblebee'. Write postcards from and to fairytale characters, e.g. Goldilocks to Baby Bear.

K – Kissing and Other Things Best Avoided – draw up a list of embarrassing things parents do – and a list for children too. Perform 'Hugger Mugger' using a strong, rhythmic chant and add in actions!

L – Love, Death, War and Peace – turn 'The Prince and the Snail' into a picture book. Discuss the poem 'From a Distance' – write out three statements about the poem.

M – Monsters, Ghosts and Ghouls – buy a copy of the CD 'Poems out Loud' (Published by Hodder Wayland) and listen to Paul Cookson perform 'We are not alone'. Invent some more frightening creatures like the 'Spotted Pyjama Snake'.

N – Nonsense – make a list of pairs of words that are impossible opposites, e.g. soft stones, dry rain, cold flames. What would you like to be named after you – Mount Tracy?

O – Ourselves and Others – make a list of all your good points (champion sweet eater) and use this to create an advert, e.g. Buy One Pie Corbett. Unique sweet eater . . . List and advertise your most amazing inventions.

P – People and Places – turn your teachers into a group of superheroes. Use a map to write lines of poetry about local places.

Q – Queens, Kings and Historical Stuff – produce an information poster to accompany any of the poems. Hot-seat a character from a poem and interview them in your role of a journalist.

R – Rescuing the World – make an alphabet chart of all your favourite natural elements (mountains, streams, tigers, snow . . .). Write a 'Missing' poster for any endangered species.

S – Senses and Feelings – boss some of your moods about,

548

like James Berry. Make a box and write down your worst memories, feelings or fears. Screw them up and throw them into the box.

T – **Teachers** – make a list of teachers' excuses for not marking homework. What are your worst/best things in school, e.g. reading aloud in class?

U – **Unpleasant Things** – hot-seat the main character and the mum in 'The Purse'. Discuss the boy in 'Incendiary'.

V – **Viewpoints** – perform 'Wizard and Witch' or 'The Dark Avenger' using two voices. Answer each of the 'Mysteries'.

W – **Wonder** – invent your own 'secret' – where did you find it, what is it made of, what can it do, what would happen if it escaped? Make and decorate a 'magic box'. Write on a small scroll all the items that you would preserve.

X – **X-words and Wordplay** – make collections of words – soft words, loud words, funny words, sad words. Create and illustrate a 'Noise' alphabet.

Y – **Young and Old** – play the game 'Hide and seek' with small poems – by hiding the poems. On each one write a mini memory. Write a memory for an old person to share.

Z – **Zapping Aliens** – write a letter from Shemu to the Nerferhotep. Describe everyday activities (like football) through an alien's eyes.

Index of First Lines

Index of First Lines

Index of First Lines

Index of First Lines

Index of First Lines

Index of Poets

Index of Poets

Acknowledgements

The publisher would like to thank the following for permission to use copyright material:

Shanta Acharya, 'If Only I Were' from *Not This, Not That* by Shanta Acharya, Rupa & Co, India (1994), by permission of the author; **John Agard**, 'Poetry Jump Up', copyright © John Agard, 1996, and 'The Rainmaker Danced', copyright © John Agard, 1999, by permission of Caroline Sheldon Literary Agency on behalf of the author, and 'That Mouth' from *Halfcast* by John Agard, Hodder Children's Books (2004), by permission of Hodder and Stoughton Ltd; **Moniza Alvi**, 'Map of India' from *Carrying My Wife* by Moniza Alvi, Bloodaxe Books (2000), by permission of Bloodaxe Books; **Moira Andrew**, 'Lost, one Siamese cat', first published in *Cambridge Contemporary Poets*, ed. Wes Magee, Cambridge University Press (1992), by permission of the author; **Shamsun Nehar Begum**, 'Grandmother' from *First Step, First Words*, by permission of First Step; **Catherine Benson**, 'Wild Cat' and 'Easter Monday', first published in *Mice on Ice*, ed, Gaby Morgan, Macmillan Children's Books (2004), by permission of the author; **Gerard Benson**, 'Lock the Dairy Door' and 'Shaking the Branches' from *Omba Bolomba: Poems by Gerard Benson*, Smith-Doorstop (2005), 'Spring Assembly' from *To Catch an Elephant* by Gerard Benson, Smith-Doorstop (2002), 'Winter Goodbye' and 'Driving Home', by permission of the author; **James Berry**, 'Mood Manager', 'Postcard Poem: Solo' and 'Singing with Recordings' from *A Nest Full of Stars* by James Berry, Macmillan Children's Books (2002), copyright © James Berry, 2002, 'Isn't My Name Magical?' from *Isn't My Name Magical?* by James Berry, Longman (1991), copyright © James Berry, 1991, and 'Listn Big Brodda Dread, Na!' from *When I Dance* by James Berry, Hamish Hamilton Children's Books (1988), copyright © James Berry, 1988, by permission of PFD on behalf of the author; **Clare Bevan**, 'Just Doing My Job', first published in *We Three Kings*, ed. Brian Moses, Macmillan Children's Books (1988), 'The Choosy Princess' and 'Counting Rhyme for a Young Princess' from *Princess Poems* by Clare Bevan, Macmillan Children's Books (2005), 'Mermaid School' and 'The Aquarium' from *Mermaid Poems* by Clare Bevan, Macmillan Children's Books (2005), 'The Music Lesson Rap', first published in *The Rhyme Riot*, ed. Gaby Morgan, Macmillan Children's Books (2002), and 'What Am I?', first published in *Bonkers for Conkers*, ed. Gaby Morgan, Macmillan Children's Books (2003), by permission of the author; **Tracey Blance**, 'Death Slide', copyright © Tracey Blance, 2005, by permission of the author; **Valerie Bloom**, 'Autumn Gilt', 'When Granny' and 'When I Grow Up and Have Children' from *Let Me Touch the Sky* by Valerie Bloom, Macmillan Children's Books, copyright © Valerie Bloom, 2000, 'Trees on Parade' and 'For Years I Asked Uncle Harry' from *Hot Like Fire* by Valerie Bloom, Bloomsbury, copyright © Valerie Bloom, 2002, and 'First Contact' from *Whoop and Shout* by Valerie Bloom, Macmillan Children's Books, copyright © Valerie Bloom,

Acknowledgements

2003, by permission of Eddison Pearson Ltd on behalf of the author; **Dave Calder**, 'On the 13th Day of Christmas', 'Little Miss Muffet', 'Changed', 'The Ascent of Vinicombe', 'Late Worker' and 'Fishy Stories', by permission of the author; **James Carter**, 'Monday Morning', 'Who Knows About UFOs?', 'Fantasy Christmas List', 'What Will I Be When I Grow Up?', 'Amazing Inventions', 'The Amazing Adventures of Space Boy Featuring Cosmic Cat' and 'Inside', copyright © James Carter, by permission of the author, and 'The Shooting Stars' from *Cars Stars Electric Guitars* by James Carter, Walker Books (2002), copyright © James Carter, 2002, by permission of Walker Books Ltd; **Charles Causley**, 'My Mother Saw a Dancing Bear' from *Collected Poems for Children* by Charles Causley, Macmillan, by permission of David Higham Associates on behalf of the author; **Debjani Chatterjee**, 'Proverbial Logic', first published in *Albino Gecko* by Debjani Chatterjee, University of Salzburg Press (1998), and 'The Last Mountain', 'Postcard from Lilliput' and '*Mehndi* Time' from *Namaskar: New and Selected Poems* by Debjani Chatterjee, Redbeck Press (2004), by permission of the author; **Gillian Clarke**, 'The Titanic', first published in *The Whispering Room*, ed. Gillian Clarke, Kingfisher Books (1996), by permission of the author; **David Cobb**, 'Children Panicking' from *The Iron Book of British Haiku*, eds David Cobb and Martin Lucas, Iron Press (1998), by permission of the author; **Mandy Coe**, 'Sensing Mother', first published in *Sensational!*, ed. Roger McGough, Macmillan Children's Books (2004), by permission of the author; **John Coldwell**, 'A Visit to Yalding' and 'My Mum's Speedy Day', by permission of the author; **Paul Cookson**, 'He Just Can't Kick It with His Foot', 'I Would Win the Gold', 'Miss King's Kong', 'Don't Get Your Knickers in a Twist', 'Short Visit, Long Stay', 'A Sumo Wrestler Chappy', 'We Are Not Alone', 'My Uncle Percy Once Removed', 'The Big Shed', 'The Haiku Monster' and 'Ten Pin Bowling', by permission of the author; **Pie Corbett**, 'Animal Riddle', 'Midnight Streetlights', 'Early Winter Diary Poem', 'Outbreak of Peace Haiku', 'Sunday Morning Diary Poem', 'Scarecrow Christmas', 'Mysteries', 'The Wolf's Wife Speaks', 'Secret Poem' and 'The Angel', by permission of the author; **Karen Costello-McFeat**, 'My Mum Wears a Jelly Bra', first published in *How to Embarrass Grown-Ups*, ed. Paul Cookson, Macmillan Children's Books (2004), by permission of the author; **John Cotton**, 'We Are a Crystal Zoo', copyright © the Estate of John Cotton, by permission of Fred Sedgwick on behalf of the Estate of the author; **Sue Cowling**, 'Christening Gift', 'Lullaby', 'Words Behaving Badly' and 'Noisy Alphabet', by permission of the author; **June Crebbin**, 'River' from *The Crocodile Is Coming!* by June Crebbin, Walker Books (2005), copyright © June Crebbin, 2005, by permission of Walker Books Ltd; **Jan Dean**, 'Mammoth Tasks', 'Canary', 'Colouring In', 'It's Not What I'm Used To' and 'An Owl Flew In My Bedroom Once', by permission of the author; **Emily Dickinson**, '"Hope" is the thing with feathers' from *The Poems of Emily Dickinson*, ed. Thomas H. Johnson, The Belknap Press of Harvard University Press, copyright © 1951, 1955, 1979, 1983 by the President and Fellows of Harvard College, by permission of the publishers and the Trustees of Amherst College; **Peter Dixon**, 'Last Waltz', 'Fairy

Acknowledgements

Picnic', 'House Party', 'Where Do All The Teachers Go?', 'Before the Days of Noah' and 'The Collector', by permission of the author; **Berlie Doherty**, 'I Love Our Orange Tent' and 'Quieter Than Snow', and with **David Dunscombe**, 'Wizard and Witch' from *Walking on Air* by Berlie Doherty, Lions (1993), by permission of David Higham Associates on behalf of the author; **Julia Donaldson**, 'Crazy Mayonnaisy' from *Crazy Mayonnaisy Mum* by Julia Donaldson, Macmillan Children's Books (2005); 'Which Witch?' from *Princess Mirror-Belle* by Julia Donaldson, Macmillan Children's Books (2003), and 'Santa Claws', by permission of Macmillan Children's Books; **Gina Douthwaite**, 'Blow This', first published in *Nothing Tastes Quite Like a Gerbil*, ed. David Orme, Macmillan Children's Books (1996), by permission of the author, and 'Rhinos and Roses' from *What Shapes An Ape?* by Gina Douthwaite, Red Fox (2002), by permission of The Random House Group Ltd; **Carol Ann Duffy**, 'Sharp Freckles' and 'Chocs' from *Meeting Midnight* by Carol Ann Duffy (1999), and 'The Oldest Girl in the World' from *The Oldest Girl in the World* by Carol Ann Duffy (2000), by permission of Faber and Faber Ltd; **Helen Dunmore**, 'Me Missing a Party' from *Secrets* by Helen Dunmore, Bodley Head (1994), by permission of A. P. Watt Ltd on behalf of the author; **Alan Durant**, 'Boy at the Somme' and 'Your Smile', copyright © Alan Durant, 2004, by permission of The Agency (London) Ltd on behalf of the author; **Richard Edwards**, 'At Three in the Morning', 'Identifying Things', 'The Blacksmith', 'The Last Bear', 'The Spell' and 'The Word Party', by permission of the author; **Eric Finney**, 'Just a Small War', by permission of the author; **Aileen Fisher**, 'Light the Festive Candles' from *Skip Around the Year* by Aileen Fisher, copyright © Aileen Fisher, 1967, by permission of Marian Reiner on behalf of the author; **Gillian Floyd**, 'My Sister's a Monster', first published in *Monster Poems*, ed. Brian Moses, Macmillan Children's Books (2005), by permission of the author; **John Foster**, 'Who's Afraid?' from *Ghost Poems*, Oxford University Press (1991), copyright © John Foster, 1991, 'Parents!' from *Four O'Clock Friday*, Oxford University Press (1991), copyright © John Foster, 1991, 'Size-Wise' from *Climb Aboard the Poetry Plane*, Oxford University Press (2000), copyright © John Foster, 2000, and 'It's Spring Again' and 'Paying His Respects', copyright © John Foster, 2005, by permission of the author; **Bashabi Fraser**, 'Come Play with Me, it's Holi' and 'A Card for Me Mom', by permission of the author; **Katherine Gallagher**, 'Tanka' included in *The Unidentified Flying Omelette*, ed. Andrew Fusek Peters, Hodder and Stoughton, by permission of the author; **Chrissie Gittens**, 'Figure', 'When Is a Boy Not a Boy?', 'Storing Time', 'Gillian Costigan', 'The Powder Monkey' and 'The Pencil Stub', by permission of the author; **Rody Gorman**, 'Two Trains', by permission of the author; **Mick Gower**, 'Sister', by permission of the author; **Judith Green**, 'Barn Owl', 'The Pumpkin Head', 'The Day the Sun Got Stuck', 'Feeding the Aardvark' and 'Allotment', by permission of the author; **David Greygoose**, 'It's Only the Storm', by permission of Dave Ward; **Mike Harding**, 'The Cruise of the Bumblebee', by permission of the author; **David Harmer**, 'Barry's Budgie Beware', 'Divali', 'One Moment in Summer', 'At Cider Mill Farm', 'A Hot Time in the

Acknowledgements

Supermarket', 'It's Behind You', 'South to North: 1965', 'At Senlac Hill', 'Our Tree', 'The Prime Minister Is Ten Today', 'We Lost Our Teacher to the Sea' and 'The Bubble Between Two Buildings', by permission of the author; **Damian Harvey**, 'Roman Invaders', first published in *Dinos, Dodos and Other Dead Things*, ed. Brian Moses, Macmillan Children's Books (2003), by permission of the author; **Trevor Harvey**, 'Vac', first published in *Techno Talk*, ed. Trevor Harvey, Bodley Head (1994), 'A Plea from an Angel', first published in *The Rhyme Riot*, ed. Gaby Morgan, Macmillan Children's Books (2002) and 'My Heart Has Been Broken', first published in *Mice on Ice*, ed. Gaby Morgan, Macmillan Children's Books (2004), by permission of the author; **Adrian Henri**, 'Autumn' from *Dinner with the Sprats* by Adrian Henri, Methuen (1993), copyright © Adrian Henri, 1993, and 'Best Friends' from *The Phantom Lollipop Lady* by Adrian Henri, Methuen (1986), copyright © Adrian Henri, 1986, by permission of Rogers, Coleridge & White Ltd on behalf of the author; **Phoebe Hesketh**, 'No One Can Call Me' from *A Song of Sunlight* by Phoebe Hesketh, Chatto & Windus (1974), by permission of The Random House Group Ltd; **Selima Hill**, 'Who's That Knocking' from *The New Exeter Book of Riddles*, ed. Kevin Crossley-Holland and Lawrence Sail, Enitharmon Press (1999), by permission of Enitharmon Press; **Gary Hotham**, 'The Clouds Bunch Quietly', included in *Global Haiku*, eds George Swede and Randy Brooks, Iron Press (2000), by permission of the author; **Elizabeth Jennings**, 'The Secret Brother' and 'The Cabbage White Butterfly' from *New Collected Poems* by Elizabeth Jennings, Carcanet (2002), by permission of David Higham Associates on behalf of the author; **Mike Johnson**, 'Wormholes in Space' included in *Minibeasts*, ed. Brian Moses, Macmillan Children's Books (1999), 'Cold Spell', 'Missing' and 'Practical Science', by permission of the author; **Jenny Joseph**, 'Great Sun' and 'Changes' from *All the Things I See* by Jenny Joseph, Macmillan Children's Books (2000), 'The Magic of the Brain' from *Bonkers for Conkers*, ed. Gaby Morgan, Macmillan Children's Books (2003), and 'The Luck of Life' from *Mice on Ice*, ed, Gaby Morgan, Macmillan Children's Books (2004), by permission of the author; **Mike Jubb**, 'Midnight Meeting' and 'The Last Day of the School Holiday', by permission of the author; **Janina Aza Karpinska**, 'Goodbye', by permission of the author; **Jackie Kay**, 'The Moon at Knowle Hill', 'At Home Abroad', 'First and Foremost', 'Duncan Gets Expelled', 'Mrs Dungeon Brae', 'Grandpa's Soup', 'Red Running Shoes' and 'Girl Footballer', by permission of the author; **Usha Kishore**, 'Tiger' and 'Tanka' from *Masala*, ed. Debjani Chatterjee, Macmillan Children's Books (2005), by permission of the author; **David Kitchen**, 'Message on the Table' and 'The Purse', by permission of the author; **Stephen Knight**, 'The Boy Who Can't Get Out of Bed', 'January 7', 'The Long Grass' and 'Sardines' from *Sardines and Other Poems* by Stephen Knight, Young Picador (2004), by permission of Macmillan Children's Books; **Tony Langham**, 'Claws' from *Larks with Sharks*, Macmillan Children's Books (1998), and 'Sir's a Secret Agent' from *More Secret Lives of Teachers*, ed. Brian Moses, Macmillan Children's Books (1997), by permission of the author; **Dennis Lee**,

Acknowledgements

'Silverly' from *Jelly Belly* by Dennis Lee, Macmillan of Canada (1983) and Key Porter (2001), copyright © Dennis Lee, 1983, by permission of Westwood Creative Artists on behalf of the author; **Richard Leigh**, 'In the Crisp-Packet' from *The Iron Book of British Haiku*, eds David Cobb and Martin Lucas, Iron Press (1998), by permission of the author; **Patricia Leighton**, 'One Christmas Wish', first published in *Christmas Poems*, ed. Gaby Morgan, Macmillan Children's Books (2003), by permission of the author; **J. Patrick Lewis**, 'Limerick', from *The Unidentified Frying Omelette*, ed, Andrew Fusek Peters, Hodder and Stoughton, by permission of the author; **Myra Cohn Livingston**, 'Prayer for Earth' from *Flights of Fancy and Other Poems* by Myra Cohn Livingston, copyright © Myra Cohn Livingston, 1993, by permission of Marian Reiner on behalf of the Estate of the author; **Rupert Loydell**, 'The Fantasy Kid', from *The Fantasy Kid* by Rupert Loydell, Stride (1990), by permission of the author; **Roger McGough**, 'Icy Fingers' from *Good Enough To Eat* by Roger McGough, Puffin (2002), copyright © Roger McGough, 2002, 'A Good Poem' from *In the Glassroom* by Roger McGough, Jonathan Cape (1976), copyright © Roger McGough, 1976, and 'The Kleptomaniac' from *Pillow Talk* by Roger McGough, Penguin Books (1990), copyright © Roger McGough, 1990, by permission of PFD on behalf of the author; **Ian McMillan**, 'The Music I Like', 'No Bread' and 'Visiting Grandad in the Home', by permission of the author; **Lindsay MacRae**, 'From a Distance', 'The Interesting Table' and 'An Army Marches on Its Stomach', by permission of the author; **Wes Magee**, 'At the End of a School Day', 'Voices' and 'The Horrible Headmonster', copyright © Wes Magee, by permission of the author; **Trevor Millum**, 'The Dark Avenger' from *Double Talk* by Trevor Millum, Kingston Press (2002); 'In Love With an Alien' and 'Match of the Year', by permission of the author; **Adrian Mitchell**, 'Song in Space' from *Adrian Mitchell's Greatest Hits*, Bloodaxe (1997), copyright © Adrian Mitchell, 1997, 'To See a Unicorn' from *Daft As a Doughnut* by Adrian Mitchell, Orchard Books (2004), copyright © Adrian Mitchell, 2004, and 'Rat It Up' and 'Disguise' from *Another Day on Your Foot and I Would Have Died*, ed. John Agard, Macmillan Children's Books (1997), copyright ©Adrian Mitchell, 1997, by permission of PFD on behalf of the author; **Tony Mitton**, 'Moon Song' and 'Penny Piece', copyright © Tony Mitton, 2004, by permission of the author; **John Mole**, 'The Shoes' from *Catching the Spider* by John Mole, Blackie (1990), and 'Thinking of You' from *The Wonder Dish* by John Mole, Oxford University Press (2002), by permission of the author; **Michaela Morgan**, 'Ice Cream', by permission of the author; **Brian Moses**, 'Our Ditch', 'Tasting the Sea', 'The River Don', 'Kirk Deighton', 'Giant's Eye View', 'Dear Yuri', 'America's Gate', 'The I-Spy Book of Teachers', 'How Teachers Leave School Each Evening', 'The Fear', 'Billy's Coming Back', 'Playing With Stars' and 'A Feather From an Angel' from *Taking Out the Tigers*, Macmillan Children's Books (2005), copyright © Brian Moses, 2005, 'What Teachers Wear in Bed', 'Aliens Stole My Underpants', 'Licking Toads' and 'The Lost Angels' from *Don't Look at Me In That Tone of Voice*, Macmillan Children's Books (1998), copyright © Brian Moses, 1998,

Acknowledgements

'Days' and 'The Snake's Revenge' from *Barking Back at Dogs*, Macmillan Children's Books (2000), 'Lovey-Dovey' and 'The Ghoul School Bus' from *Knock Down Ginger and Other Poems*, Cambridge University Press (1994), copyright © Brian Moses, 1994, 'Righting Wrongs' and 'White Horse', first published in this collection, copyright © Brian Moses, 2005 and, with Pie Corbett, 'Lost Kitty in New York City' from *Taking Out the Tigers*, Macmillan Children's Books (2005), copyright © Brian Moses and Pie Corbett, by permission of the author; **Marlene Mountain**, 'one fly everywhere the heat' included in *Global Haiku*, eds George Swede and Randy Brooks, Iron Press, by permission of the author; **Frances Nagle**, 'Get Your Things Together, Hayley', by permission of the author; **Judith Nicholls**, 'Japheth's Notes: A Fragment' from *Magic Mirror* by Judith Nicholls, Faber and Faber Ltd (1985), copyright © Judith Nicholls, 1985, and 'Spring Magic', 'In Praise of Aunties', 'Horace the Horrid', 'Stirring Times' and 'Football, as Understood by a Martian', copyright © Judith Nicholls, 2005, by permission of the author; **Grace Nichols**, 'Give Yourself a Hug' from *Give Yourself a Hug* by Grace Nichols, A & C Black (1994), copyright © Grace Nichols, 1994, 'Me and the Moon' from *Everybody Got a Gift* by Grace Nichols, A & C Black (2005), copyright © Grace Nichols, 2005, and 'Mistress Cooper', by permission of Curtis Brown Ltd on behalf of the author; **David Orme**, 'Larks With Sharks', 'Perishing', 'Mary Celeste', 'Horribly Thin Poem', 'Hogging Hedgehogs' and 'Football in the Rain', copyright © David Orme, by permission of the author; **Gareth Owen**, 'Summer Farm', 'Megan's Day', 'Shell', 'Jack in the Sky', 'Wellingtons', 'Star Gazing', 'Universal Zoo', 'Jemima' and 'Den to Let' from *Collected Poems* by Gareth Owen, Macmillan Children's Books (2000), copyright © Gareth Owen, 2000, by permission of Rogers, Coleridge & White Ltd on behalf of the author; **Brian Patten**, 'Dear Mum' from *Thawing Frozen Frogs* by Brian Patten, Viking (1990), copyright © Brian Patten, 1990, and 'The Secret Rhyme for Orange' from *Juggling with Gerbils* by Brian Patten, Puffin Books (2000), copyright © Brian Patten, 2000, by permission of Rogers, Coleridge and White on behalf of the author; **Andrew Fusek Peters**, 'Sensational Day', first published in *Sensational!*, ed. Roger McGough, Macmillan Children's Books (2004), 'Fire at Night' first published in *The Works 3*, ed. Paul Cookson, Macmillan Children's Books (2004), 'The Teflon Terror' first published in *Spectacular Spooks*, ed. Brian Moses, Macmillan Children's Books (2001), 'Betrayal' first published in *Poems with Attitude Uncensored* by Andrew Fusek Peters and Polly Peters, Hodder and Stoughton (2002), and 'The Mysterious Employment of God', by permission of the author; **Gervase Phinn**, 'Reading Round the Class', 'A Proper Poet' and 'All Creatures', by permission of the author; **Tim Pointon**, 'Teasing Ghosts', first published in *Spectacular Spooks*, ed. Brian Moses, Macmillan Children's Books (2001), by permission of the author; **Irene Rawnsley**, 'Night Train' from *Night Poems*, ed. John Foster, Oxford University Press (1991), and 'Treasure Trove' from *Ask a Silly Question* by Irene Rawnsley, Methuen Children's Books (1988), by permission of the author; **James Reeves**, 'Fireworks' from *Complete Poems for*

Acknowledgements

Children by James Reeves, 'Classic Mammoth', copyright © James Reeves Estate, by permission of Laura Cecil Literary Agency on behalf of the Estate of the author; **John Rice**, 'Castle to Be Built in the Woods' and 'A Minute to Midnight' from *Guzzling Jelly with Giant Gorbelly* by John Rice, Macmillan Children's Books (2004), by permission of the author; **Philip Ridley**, 'The Prince and the Snail', by permission of A. P. Watt Ltd on behalf of the author; **Coral Rumble**, 'The First Bit', 'The World Is Dark When All My Friends Grow Cold' and 'Cornered', by permission of the author; **Vernon Scannell**, 'The Day That Summer Died', 'Nettles', 'Incendiary', 'The Magic Show' and 'Grannie', by permission of the author; **Fred Sedgwick**, 'Some Other Ark', 'Thaw', 'After Giacometti', 'Victoria's Poem' and 'Home', copyright © Fred Sedgwick, by permission of the author; **Andrea Shavick**, 'Grandma Was Eaten by a Shark' and 'Auntie Betty Thinks She's Batgirl', by permission of the author; **James Simmons**, 'A Birthday Poem for Rachel' from *Poems 1956–1986* by James Simmons, The Gallery Press (1986), by permission of The Gallery Press and the Estate of the author; **Matt Simpson**, 'Summery', 'Grandad's Garden', 'Reincarnation' and 'By the River', by permission of the author; **Roger Stevens**, 'We Are the Year Six Boys', 'On Mother's Day', 'Escape Plan', 'Mums', 'We Are the Year Six Girls', 'Walking the Dog Seems Like Fun to Me', 'Sonnet Number One', 'When Your Face Doesn't Fit', 'To Mother Earth', 'Grandma', 'Grandma's Jigsaw Puzzle', 'My Stepdad Is an Alien' and 'Cat Message', by permission of the author; **George Swede**, 'In the Dentist's Waiting Room', by permission of the author; **Matthew Sweeney**, 'Cows on the Beach' and 'Up on the Roof' from *Up on the Roof* by Matthew Sweeney (2001) by permission of Faber and Faber Ltd; **Marian Swinger**, 'The First Christmas', first published in *We Three Kings*, ed. Brian Moses, Macmillan Children's Books (1998), 'The Picnic', first published in *The Horrible Headmonster*, ed. Adrian Henri et al, Macmillan Children's Books (2003), 'Notes in Class', first published in *Bonkers for Conkers*, ed. Gaby Morgan, Macmillan Children's Books (2003), and 'Tiger Eyes', by permission of the author; **George Szirtes**, 'The Rainbow Mystery', by permission of the author; **Nick Toczek**, 'They're Out There', 'There's a Dragon in the Cellar' and 'The Dragon Who Ate Our School' from *Dragons!* by Nick Toczek, Macmillan Children's Books (2005), and 'The Great Escape', 'Staff Meeting' and 'If I Were the Leader', by permission of the author; **Barrie Wade**, 'Learning' from *Rainbow* by Barrie Wade, Oxford University Press, by permission of the author; **Celia Warren**, 'Dead As a Dodo' and 'A Liking for a Viking' from *Vikings Don't Wear Pants* by Roger Stevens and Celia Warren, Kings England Press (2001), by permission of the author; **John Whitworth**, 'The Cheer-up Song', by permission of the author; **Kit Wright**, 'Hugger Mugger' and 'The Magic Box', by permission of the author.

Every effort has been made to trace the copyright holders but if any have been inadvertently overlooked the publishers will be pleased to make the necessary arrangement at the first opportunity.